Danger on the
Streets of Gold

Danger on the Streets of Gold

Adoniram Judson

Irene Howat

CF4·K

Dedication: For Elinor

© Copyright 2001 Christian Focus Publications
Reprinted 2007

ISBN 978-1-85792-660-6

Published by
Christian Focus Publications,
Geanies House, Fearn, Tain, Ross-shire,
IV20 1TW, Scotland, U.K.
Tel: 01862 871011
Fax: 01862 871699

www.christianfocus.com
email: info@christianfocus.com

Cover design by Alister Macinnes
Cover illustration by Peter Gibson

Printed and bound in Denmark
by Nørhaven Paperback A/S

Contents

Young Mr Judson 7

About turn! 19

Adventures at sea 31

La Belle Creol 43

Early days 53

Goings and comings 65

The Golden Presence 77

Ava, at last 89

Death Prison 101

Oung-pen-la 111

A second happiness 123

The Golden Shore 135

Thinking Further Topics 147

Time Line 156

Young Mr Judson

Having hammered in the very last nail, the carpenter climbed down the ladder to admire his handiwork. The sign was absolutely straight. It looked good. Picking up his ladder and toolbag, he turned and left. A young man standing nearby looked up at the newly erected sign and smiled.

'Plymouth Independent Academy,' Adoniram Judson read to the puppy at his side. 'Who'd have thought I'd be opening a school for the intelligent young of the great state of Massachusetts! I wonder if I'm the youngest headmaster in the area. There can't be many nineteen-year-olds with schools of their own!'

The puppy, recognising his master's happy voice, wagged his tail in agreement. Adoniram knelt on the grass. 'Let's shake hands on the school's success,' he said. 'Give me a paw.'

Obediently the puppy sat down and raised a paw. He tried to combine this with wagging his tail in delight at the attention he was receiving, and just about managed.

Adoniram laughed. 'If my pupils all learn as quickly as you do the school will be a great success.'

'You must be very proud of your boy,' a friend told

Mr and Mrs Judson. 'He's a real credit to you both. I hear he's writing books as well as running his school.'

Adoniram's father, Rev Adoniram Judson, smiled, but had no time to answer before his wife spoke proudly of their eldest child. 'That's right! He's already written *Elements of English Grammar* and he's almost finished *The Young Lady's Arithmetic*.'

Their visitor nodded to the Judsons but smiled to himself. 'That's a young man who ought to get a life,' he thought.

And that's just what Adoniram was thinking too.

'I'm giving up the school,' he told his parents quite soon afterwards.

Mrs Judson, had been aware that her son had become restless in his work. 'You've just had a bad week,' she assured him. 'Things always look at their worst on Friday evenings. You wait and see, you'll feel differently on Monday.'

Mr Judson watched the contortions on Adoniram's face. 'And what would you do if you were to give up the school?' he asked.

The young man, who had expected a tirade about irresponsibility and security and other such things as didn't interest him, suddenly realised to his horror that his father expected him to say that he wanted to close the school in order to train to be a minister! His mind went into a spin. His stomach heaved with apprehension, and he thought he was going to have to leave the room. Then his words all came out in a rush.

'I can't bear the thought of teaching for the rest of my life, and...' he looked at his father.

The older man's eyes lit up, hope gleaming out of them, 'You'll train to be a minister?'

Adoniram felt sick. But he knew there was no going back. 'No I can't,' he said, his voice quavering. 'I respect what you believe and in a way I admire what you do, but it's not for me. I can't preach the Bible because I don't believe it's God's Word. It's no different from any other book. It's just another book written by men for men. And,' he gulped at the prospect of the reaction he expected when he made his final statement, 'and I don't believe that Jesus was the son of God either. He was certainly a good man, but that's all he was, a man.'

Mr Judson's face fell. He sank to his seat, and Adoniram heard the whispered words, 'Part of me has just died, part of me has just died.'

Adoniram's mother couldn't bear it. 'I'm sure you could make a living writing books,' she said hopefully, but with absolutely no conviction. However, Adoniram grasped at the straw his mother had unwittingly held out.

'Yes,' he said. 'That's what I want to do. I want to be a writer ...' and now that he had started talking he couldn't stop himself. 'I want to write interesting things, not school books. I want to write stories and plays for the theatre. I want to travel, I'll join a touring theatre company and I'll write new plays for it to perform.'

For the six days that followed Mr Judson heaved

heavy sighs. Adoniram avoided going past his study door because each time he did he heard his father pleading in prayer for his soul. But his mother was even worse - always behind him, weeping, praying, begging, until her son could take no more. Still a little short of twenty years old, Adoniram packed his few things together and rode off to Albany where he boarded a boat for New York. That trip contributed just a little chip to history, for he travelled on the first successful steamboat. It was called the *Clermont*.

The weeks that followed were all that Adoniram hoped they would be. He did join a group of travelling actors and he did write short plays for them. There was a real thrill in seeing his words come to life on the stage, but less excitement in seeing the empty seats where the audience should have been. And for a young man brought up strictly there was even a kick to be had in living like a vagabond, and in finding lodgings wherever he could, only to get up before the landlord in the morning and leave without paying. But it was not long until Adoniram realised that writing for the stage wasn't what he thought it would be, that the loud laughter he and his friends shared was often hollow, and that the life of a strolling player wasn't for him. Buttoning himself up against the 'I told you so' he thought would meet him at the door of his home, he headed in that direction.

'Young Mr Judson!' the maid said, as she opened the door. 'How you've grown!'

'Is my uncle at home?' Adoniram asked. 'I'm on my way back home from New York and I wondered if I might stay overnight.'

Opening the door wide, the woman explained that his uncle was away but that he was very welcome to a bed. 'There's a young preacher here while your uncle is travelling. I'm sure you'll enjoy each other's company.'

Judson swallowed hard. A keen young preacher getting at him was just what he didn't need. But if he wanted a free bed he had no choice but risk it.

'Tell me about yourself,' the preacher invited, as they sat beside the fire after their evening meal.

And, much to Adoniram's surprise, he found himself telling this comfortable stranger about his disappointments and doubts, his hopes and his fears. Far from preaching, the minister just spoke about himself as Adoniram had spoken, and it was somehow more powerful than any sermon young Judson had ever heard. The young preacher spoke of Jesus as one of his friends in a way that set Adoniram thinking. Though he would have enjoyed the preacher's company for longer, Adoniram left the following day for the next leg of his journey home.

'Yes, I've a room you can have,' an innkeeper said that evening when Adoniram knocked at his door. 'But I'm afraid you might be disturbed. There's a young man in the next room to it who is very ill. Dying, I should think. Sometimes he moans in his sleep. But take it or leave it, that's the only room I've got left.'

'I'll take it. Maybe he'll have a decent night and we'll both get some sleep.'

But the ill young man had a terrible night. He cried out and wept. It was awful to hear it. And Adoniram had hardly any sleep at all. In order to blank out what was happening in the next room he lay on his side, pulled a pillow over his head, hauled the blanket on top, and thought over his life to date. He had a vivid imagination, and before long the distressing sounds from next door were masked by memories. And so long as he concentrated on his memories he could forget the poor young man.

'What's my very earliest memory?' he asked himself. 'I know! I remember when my sister Abigail was born. I wasn't quite three then. And I remember worrying that the baby would be given my striped blanket, and I knew I couldn't sleep without it. Even when I was six and my little brother was born, I still used that blanket as a comforter.' His mind wandered. 'I wonder what would comfort that poor soul?' he asked himself, hearing the groans through the wall. Then he concentrated on his memories again. 'How I loved being in father's study,' he said aloud but quietly. That helped to drown out the distressing noises. 'I was fascinated by his quill pen and glass ink-pot. And I loved watching him scatter fine sand on his writing to help it dry.'

Quite out of the blue a scene flashed into Adoniram's mind. It was 1791. He was three years old, and his father was on a preaching trip.

'Would you like to give Papa a surprise when he comes home?' his mother asked.

Greatly excited at the thought of the surprise, the boy followed his mother into the sitting-room where, with splendid patience, she taught her tiny son to read a chapter of the Bible. Judson felt his heart aching as he remembered his father's return home and his disbelief turning to pride when the chapter was read to him by his three-year-old son.

'I wonder if the Bible would help that poor man,' Adoniram thought. He shook his head. 'It's none of my business. Now where was I?'

Memory followed memory - of the pigs and hens in the back garden, of the maid who taught him to make all the animal noises, of games played and puzzles done. 'Puzzles,' he said aloud, and grinned.

'I was eight or nine,' he remembered, 'when I did the Enigma puzzle in the newspaper and sent it off to the editor without a stamp. However, the postman recognised my writing and gave it back to Papa. I suppose that was fair enough though, after all, the newspaper would have had to pay the postage if it had arrived. I remember Father's face when he opened the letter and saw how well I'd done the puzzle, and that I'd got the right answer too! I could hardly believe it when he was so impressed that he promised to buy me a puzzle book of my own. And I can still recall the disappointment when it was a book of arithmetic problems he bought! Poor Papa, he never could get things quite right.'

The noise from the neighbouring room was reaching a crescendo. Adoniram spoke out his memories louder to try to drown it out. 'I suppose he did get it right sometimes,' he admitted, 'like when he took me to the harbour to see the ships coming and going. When we lived at Salem the boats carried exciting cargoes: silks and spices, sometimes even live monkeys. It was a pity Papa moved to churches in Braintree, then Plymouth. Cod fishing boats was all Plymouth rose to, and the smell of them put me off going to the harbour at all!'

His memory settled on his primary school days. 'I never saw mathematics as work,' he recalled. 'I just enjoyed it. But I liked most things really. I must have seemed a terrible swot to the other boys. I loved languages - they are just like puzzles. It's fun seeing what English words came from Latin and Greek words. Papa laughed so much when I tried to play the piano and pretended I was a great musician called Cakos Phonos, the Greek for loud noise! Languages fascinate me. Maybe I could find a career based on languages. I'll have to think about that.'

'Papa uses words well,' Adoniram said, still struggling to block out the terrible scene he could picture in the adjoining room. 'He told us wonderful stories when we were children. Why was it then that he was so dull when he was preaching? What do I remember about his sermons?' He thought back, but it was the church building that came into his mind, not what his father had said. Despite the noise next door, Judson found himself smiling. 'Those old box pews were splendid when I was small. If I wanted to see Papa I climbed up on a stool to look over. But if I didn't want to see him, or I didn't want him to see me, all I had to do was get off the stool and I was out of sight. What games my imagination conjured up using the foot-warmers in the pew! They were boats going to faraway places, or snow shoes for tramping high up in the mountains, or they were four-poster beds for me to snuggle down in. I even remember taking little wooden model horses into church once and pretending that the foot-warmer was their stable. Mama wasn't best pleased when she saw them!'

'I was about fourteen when I had my serious phase,' Judson remembered aloud. 'A year sick and off school saw to that. No wonder I wanted to be a minister then, I was so bored!' Then Adoniram realised that hadn't been true at all. Yes, he had wanted to be a famous minister of a huge church, but he hadn't been bored, the books in his father's study had seen to that. 'I soon caught up at school,' he recalled, 'and headed off to Rhode Island College at Providence when I was sixteen years and six days old. It was there I met Jacob Eames, and he opened my eyes.' There was silence from the room next door, and Adoniram relaxed into thought of college life. 'What laughs we had! What discussions! Jacob was the first serious thinker I knew who didn't believe in God and who built his life on a whole different set of ideas. I'd just accepted what I'd been taught till then, but Jacob helped me to challenge all that Christian thinking and to come out the other end knowing I could face life head on without needing the help of any god. And it works,' he concluded. 'I know it works because I've proved it for myself. Good old Jacob!' Judson's mind rambled over his college years.

He pictured his teachers and his friends. 'What a funny thing life is,' he concluded. 'When we were at college our friendships seemed as though they would last for ever and now I don't know where most of my friends are, not even Jacob. I don't know where he is, but I do know where he's not,' Judson smiled at the thought. 'He's not in church on Sundays!'

The night hours passed slowly. Having been disturbed by the noises in the next room, Adoniram now found himself needing to hear them to assure himself that his neighbour was still in the land of the living. But nothing came, and the silence oppressed the young man as much as the noise had unnerved him. He tried not to think about death, but he couldn't help it. 'What would happen to me if I died?' he asked himself. But he had no answer. Was there a heavenly home for those who trusted in Jesus? Would there really be a day of judgement, and if there was, how would he be judged? Did hell exist? And was that where he was heading? All these questions rattled around in his mind, tormenting him in the uneasy silent darkness. He could hear his father's voice telling him that everything he had been taught from the Bible was true. He could hear Jacob Eames' dismissal of the very idea. And the hours wore on. 'Was ever a night as long as this one?' he demanded of the early dawn, 'or as disturbing?' It was nearly time to get up when Judson eventually fell asleep. And all was quiet in the room next door.

'How's the fellow who was ill?' Adoniram asked, as he paid his account before leaving.

The man looked up. 'He's dead.'

Young Judson could imagine the moment of death. There had been moaning and groaning, cries and tears, louder … and louder. Then silence. That terrible silence. Despite himself, Adoniram wondered if the dead man had met his Maker, if he had met his judge. Shaking himself free of the thought, he took his change from the innkeeper.

'What was his name?' Judson asked, more to escape his thoughts than out of any real interest.

'His name was Jacob Eames,' the landlord said. 'A young man like yourself. Jacob Eames would have been just about your age.'

About turn!

Jacob Eames, the same confident outgoing young man, so sure of his ideas and certain in his belief that there was no God. Yet in the end Jacob's screams had said it all.

'I don't know what Jacob died of,' Adoniram said to himself as he began his journey home again, 'but I do know that his screams weren't the sounds of someone who was ready to die.'

Adoniram began to run. He had to do something with the frantic energy that possessed him. But it alternated with a terrible heaviness that made it hard even to walk. 'If God's real what did Jacob have to say to him? God wouldn't be very impressed by being told he didn't exist. Does that mean Jacob's in hell?' The energy hit him again and he ran and ran, trying to run away from himself, from his grief, from memories of Jacob's last hours and of all he could have done for his friend and had not. Then it was as though a plug was pulled and every ounce of strength leaked out of him.

Sitting on a low branch of a tree at the side of the road, Adoniram Judson faced the dark reality that even if he had known it was his friend who was dying, even if he had been with Jacob until the very end, he had nothing, absolutely nothing, that would have been of any comfort to him. And he had the honesty and insight to realise that if their roles had been reversed, Jacob would have been no use to him either. Anxious as Adoniram had been to leave home, now he couldn't get back there quickly enough. As a young man his father's certainties had annoyed him intensely. But over the night that had just dragged past Adoniram Judson had grown up, and what he most needed now was to be certain that, when his time came, death wouldn't find him as unready as it had found Jacob Eames.

If Adoniram expected a rough time when he got home he must have been surprised by the tenderness of the welcome he received, and it wasn't just because there were visitors in the house. Mr and Mrs Judson had prayed every day and many times a day that their son would come safely home and that he would come to faith in Jesus. The first part of their prayer had been answered and they were content to leave the second part in the hands of God.

The two visitors were there to discuss with Mr Judson a new Bible college they were setting up. Inevitably it wasn't long before one of them, quite unaware that Adoniram wasn't a Christian, tried to persuade him to go there as a student.

'I don't think that's the place for me,' the young man told them. 'I'm thinking about going to Boston to work.'

If the Judsons felt misgivings about that, they held their peace. They were aware of changes in their son and felt more easy about him going away again.

Adoniram did go to Boston and found a job. At first he enjoyed it, but very soon a terrible restlessness developed in him and he couldn't settle to anything. Six weeks after arriving in Boston he packed up his things and went home.

'I've decided to go to this new Bible College,' he explained to his parents on his return. 'Maybe I'll find what I'm looking for there.'

And after he left the room, Mr and Mrs Judson knelt beside their chairs and prayed that he would indeed find the answer to his question, and that he would find that the answer was Jesus Christ.

The young man started college with many doubts and questions, but as the weeks went past he began to find some answers. Then, in the winter of his twentieth year, he became a Christian.

'There were no blinding lights,' he told a fellow student. 'There was nothing dramatic and sudden, just a quiet realisation that the Bible is God's Word, and that it must be true because God doesn't tell lies. And if the Bible is true, then Jesus is God's son and only those who put their trust in him can have their sins forgiven and go to heaven.'

'Wow! That's quite a sermon,' his friend said. 'We'll make a preacher of you yet!'

Adoniram could picture himself as a preacher, standing in the pulpit week by week preaching lively and interesting sermons to a big and attentive American congregation. Then he felt a twinge of conscience. 'If my father has been content to work in small congregations all of his ministry, why should I have a big church? Fifty years from now probably nobody will even remember him so why on earth should I think that I'm important!'

There was a student prayer meeting that evening, and Adoniram and several others gathered together for it.

'Let's make up a list of things to pray for,' the leader said.

'First let's ask God to bless the college.'

'And the churches we all attend.'

'Please pray for my parents. My father is unwell,' one student told the group.

Another added, 'I think we should ask the Lord to help us to be good students now and faithful ministers when we settle in our churches.'

'And that we should be humble,' Adoniram said, 'wanting to show people Jesus rather than ourselves.' After he said the words, Judson prayed silently that God would take away thoughts of being a famous preacher in a wealthy church in a big American city.

'What are you reading now?' Adoniram's friend asked him. 'You always have your nose in a book!'

There was no response. The man tapped Judson on the shoulder. He jumped!

'I asked what you were reading and you were so engrossed you didn't even hear me.'

Adoniram looked at his friend with eyes that were

fiery with excitement. 'Sit down and listen to this,' he instructed.

Flicking back over the pages, he found where he was looking for and read, *Burma is a heathen land, though not totally closed to the gospel. The people are sophisticated and many are highly educated. There is one missionary in the land of Burma, and he is a Roman Catholic priest. No part of the Bible has yet been translated into Burmese.*

He snapped the book shut. 'What an opportunity! Doesn't that make you want to go right out there and tell them about Jesus?'

Judson's friend sat down. 'You're living in cloud cuckoo land,' he said, 'and you're letting your imagination run away with you. Do you really picture yourself as the first non-Catholic missionary to Burma, the first American missionary ever?'

Adoniram was puzzled by the reaction. 'Someone's got to be first,' he said. 'What's so special about that?'

When he wasn't at lectures or preparing for exams Judson could always be found in the library. He read every missionary story he could find, and every book about Burma.

'Is that what God is wanting me to do?' he asked himself, 'or am I just looking for adventure?' Taking up his pen, he wrote down a list of pros and cons.

For going to Burma:
I want to serve God wherever he asks me to go.
I like languages and am quite good at them.
I could translate the Bible into Burmese.

23

I like grammar and that would help me learn Burmese.
I've already written a book on grammar and I could write another in Burmese. Future missionaries could use it to learn the language.
I love adventures.
Against going to Burma:
Nobody from our church has ever gone there.
Americans don't go abroad as missionaries. It's British people who do that, and Roman Catholic priests.
No one would pay me so what would I live on?
It would mean leaving my family, perhaps for ever.
I'm the eldest son and should be responsible for my parents when they are old.

On a snowy day when all these things were rumbling around in Adoniram's mind, he went out for a walk in the woods. Did he hear the words in his ears or in his heart? He never knew the answer to that question, but he certainly heard them.

'Go into all the world and preach the gospel.'

After his walk he found his list of pros and cons and tore it up. What did the cons matter when God had spoken? And the list of pros that were in his mind were now different.

For being a missionary:
God has called me.
God will provide for all my needs.
God will go with me wherever I go.
God will take care of my parents.

The snow was still on the ground when Adoniram went home for his winter holiday. He knew he would have to tell his parents what he was thinking and he was fairly sure that, although they would be surprised, they would accept that if God had called their son to go overseas, he had no choice but to go. There was an air of suppressed excitement when he arrived and, when the subject of his future came up, he was a little bemused by the looks which passed between his parents, brother and sister.

'My future now seems quite clear to me,' Adoniram told them.

His father beamed. 'I thought you'd be pleased. But how did you hear?'

The young man's puzzled expression seemed to entertain his brother.

'God showed me through missionary books and especially through a book about Burma.'

It was his family's turn to look puzzled.

Adoniram went on, 'and then he spoke to me, telling me to go into all the world and preach the gospel.'

'But what about Boston?' It was his mother who spoke.

'What about it?'

Mr Judson decided the time had come to clear up the confusion. 'You're going to be offered the post of assistant minister in one of the biggest churches in Boston. Your teachers speak highly of you, and it's on their recommendation that the offer is being made. I can't tell you how pleased your mother and I are.'

Mrs Judson looked somewhere between laughter and tears, and not quite sure which was appropriate.

Adoniram swallowed hard. 'I'm sorry to disappoint you, but I'm afraid I'll have to turn it down. God has shown me clearly that he wants me to go overseas for him.'

The bubble of suppressed excitement burst. The Judson family was appalled at the prospect of missionary service. It was so much not a part of American thinking at that time that it seemed plain madness to them.

Adoniram returned to college expecting the same frosty reception. But a pleasant surprise awaited him - four other students were also considering missionary service!

'Let's go for a walk,' one of the four suggested. 'We can walk and talk.'

So engrossed were they in missionary discussion that they didn't notice the first few spots of rain, nor did they hear the distant rumble of thunder.

'We can shelter behind that haystack,' Adoniram said, when they could ignore the rain no longer. The young men raced towards the farmyard but were thoroughly soaked by the time they got there.

Crouching at the foot of the haystack, they prayed for missions overseas as the thunder rumbled all round them and the rain lashed down. They hadn't noticed the rain coming on, and they didn't notice it going off. Their prayers were crossing continents and what was happening right where they were didn't seem very important.

Two years later the five young men formed a little missionary group. Soon afterwards two other students joined them. Much of their talk was about what needed to be done overseas, but some of it was about the very ordinary subject of money.

'I think you should write to the London Missionary Society,' Adoniram was told at one of their meetings. 'Perhaps it will support us, for it looks as though the church in America won't.'

That afternoon he put pen to paper, asking if there was any possibility of the Society supporting missionaries, especially to *any part of the eastern continent*. He ended the letter by *wishing myself to receive a letter from you immediately*.

Meanwhile the group tried to encourage support for mission in their own denomination. There was much discussion on the subject.

'It's not part of our tradition to be sending people to distant countries.'

'But maybe it should be.'

'You hear terrible things from these heathen lands. It wouldn't be safe to send men there.'

'In any case, we need them to be ministers here in America.'

'We'd better not attempt to stop God,' one highly respected church leader said, at the end of a meeting on the subject.

That swayed the decision and the Board of Commissioners for Foreign Missions was founded. And on that very same day Adoniram Judson fell in love.

He was invited to lunch at the home of Dean John Hasseltine, and the meal was not nearly so memorable as the girl who served the pie. Ann (who was known as Nancy) was the Dean's daughter. Born in 1789, she was eleven years younger than Adoniram.

Judson enthused about the young woman to his friends that evening. 'She has olive skin and dark brown sparkling eyes, and she's a Christian, a dear sweet devoted believer.'

'Anything else to recommend her?' one of his friends asked.

'Yes, she's a teacher.'

There was no doubt about it, Adoniram had fallen in love.

The months that followed were full. Adoniram studied hard, and did everything else hard too. He had daily cold sponge baths to try to harden his body for missionary service, and he did deep breathing exercises. He took long walks whatever the weather. And he got to know Ann. That bit was easy.

When he was sure of his feelings for her, he wrote to Dean Hasseltine indicating his interest in both Ann and missionary service. The dean left the response to his daughter, though one of his friends had plenty to say on the matter. 'I would tie my daughter to the bedpost rather than let her go on such a hare-brained venture.'

After much thought and prayer, Ann wrote her reply to Adoniram's proposal of marriage.

Jesus is faithful, and his promises are precious. Were that not the case I should despair, especially as no other female has, to my knowledge, ever left the shores of America to spend her life among the heathen, nor do I know if I shall have a single female companion. But I dare not decline an offer I believe to be God's will even though many are ready to call it a wild romantic undertaking.

Adventures at sea

On 11th January 1811, Ann waved goodbye to her fiancé, and watched as his ship, *The Packet*, eased out of the dock taking him on the first stage of his long journey to London for discussions with the London Missionary Society. As the days passed she would smile as she pictured him busy studying his Hebrew Old Testament, translating parts into English, others into Latin. Ann was good at languages, but for Adoniram it was a passion.

For a while what she imagined was happening on board *The Packet* was in fact fairly accurate. That was until a ship was sighted in the distance one morning as the sun came up. The first Adoniram was aware that something was wrong was when he heard the word 'pirate' being whispered from ship's boy to ship's boy. Looking up from his books, he saw terror on their small faces.

'What's wrong?' he asked the two who were nearest him.

'That's *L'Invincible Napoleon*, and it's a pirate ship,' one boy answered. 'And they say pirates kidnap ship's boys then work them to death.'

Adoniram didn't know what to say. He'd spent much of his childhood on the sea coast, and pirate adventures had featured in many of his games.

There was no time for further conversation. The captain of *The Packet* barked orders to crew members, to the few passengers on board and to the boys. Sailors rushed around the deck. The orders were given to take up arms and a sea battle raged. By then the boats were alongside and men jumped from one to the other. There was hand-to-hand fighting, and knives flashed in the sunlight, some of them dripping red with blood. Dead sailors from both ships were kicked into the sea, and Judson saw at least one live man go over and struggle as he sank. Pirates hacked at the sails of *The Packet*, trying to disable her, and the sailors fought furiously to prevent them. But it was an uneven struggle from the very beginning. The pirates were fighting men, the crew of *The Packet* were sailors. The battle raged for nearly two hours, but there was never a real contest. It was just a matter of time. When all was quiet Judson and a number of sailors were on the *L'Invincible Napoleon*, prisoners in the hold. Bruised and battered from the battle, Adoniram thought of Ann. He thought of the plans they had made together and of the mission work they had looked forward to doing. That was when he decided that he might as well go on preparing to go overseas with her. What else was there to do anyway?

Taking out his Hebrew Old Testament and a note book, Judson began to translate some verses from Hebrew to Latin.

'What's that?' the pirate ship's doctor asked in French.

Adoniram didn't understand what was said, but he held out the books anyway. The doctor, a well-educated man, recognised the words in Latin and the two of them found they were able to talk in that long dead language!

'Are you a priest?'

'No, but I'm training to be a missionary. Where are we going and what will happen to us?' Judson asked.

'We're heading for France where you'll be put in prison until it's decided what to do with you. You'll probably get out of this mess all right, most Americans who are captured do.'

That night Judson was taken from the hold.

'I spoke to the captain about you,' the doctor said, by way of explanation. 'You'll not be put back down there.'

'Thank you,' Judson replied, still in Latin, 'I'm grateful to you.'

Because nobody else on board knew the language they had no idea what the two men were talking about. Instead of eating thin porridge in the hold with the other prisoners, Judson ate a good meal at the captain's table and was given a cabin for the rest of the voyage.

After a brief stop at a Spanish port, *L'Invincible Napoleon* sailed north to France where it found a port and off-loaded its cargo of prisoners, Adoniram included.

'Where are we being taken?' he asked the doctor in Latin as he left the boat.

'To the town prison,' was the reply. 'But call out that

33

you're an American. If anyone understands you they may be able to get help.'

And that's what Adoniram did. As he was marched past a group of people, a man came up to him and said, in an American accent, that he'd try to help him. And when he was locked in a cell with many others, Judson wondered what his fellow countryman could possibly do.

Some time later the cell door opened and the prison officer brought in the tall American. He was wearing a full length black cloak that flowed behind him as he moved. Walking round the cell, he looked first at one man then another, each time saying, 'He's no friend of mine,' or, 'I don't know him.'

'Go for it,' he whispered to Adoniram as he hustled past in the darkness of the prison, swinging his cloak behind him. Judson ducked under the cloak, fell into step behind the tall American, and they walked out of the cell as one!

'That's my first time, and I hope my last time, in prison,' Adoniram told his rescuer when they had reached safety. 'It's not an experience I'd like to repeat.'

It was weeks before Judson finally got to England and met with the Council of the London Missionary Society.

'Would you consider helping four of us to get to the east as missionaries?' he asked the men who interviewed him. 'We have some funding, but we'll need more support than we can raise in America.'

The Council discussed the possibility.

'Tell us more about yourselves,' a kindly man asked. 'That will help us come to a decision.'

Judson gave a little of his own history, then told the men about his student friends.

'And there will be our wives too,' he concluded.

There was a sudden cold silence in the room.

'You are married?' the chairman asked in an amazed tone. 'You are considering taking young women to India or Burma!'

'No, I'm not married,' Adoniram explained.

He could feel the relief all around him.

'But I am engaged to be married.'

The discussions were heavy and heated. Wives were obviously a problem. But just as Adoniram was expecting a totally negative response, the Council came to the decision that they would provide some funding for the work, the rest to be found in America.

Eight months after leaving Adoniram arrived back in New York with the good news of financial backing from London for the missionary venture.

'I've something I must do on my way home,' he thought, as he set out on the last lap of his journey to Boston.

Knocking at the doors of inns he remembered, he waited for them to open.

'You won't remember me,' he said to one innkeeper after another. 'But some years ago, when I was a stupid young man, I was with a group of travelling players. We took lodgings from you, then left early in the morning without paying the bill. I'm a Christian now and I'd like to settle that account with you.'

There were several very surprised innkeepers between New York and Boston. Some remembered the occasion, others said it happened all the time. One even told Adoniram to forget it and keep the money, but he would not. He could not. His debts had to be paid.

On 5th February 1812 Adoniram Judson and Ann Hasseltine were married. The following day the new missionaries were ordained as ministers. The service concluded with a hymn written especially for the occasion. There was hardly a dry eye as it was sung.

> *Go, ye heralds of salvation;*
> *Go, and preach in heathen lands;*
> *Publish loud to every nation,*
> *What the Lord of life commands.*

> *Go, ye sisters, their companions,*
> *Soothe their cares, and wipe their tears,*
> *Angels shall in bright battalions*
> *Guard your steps and guard your fears.*

> *Landed safe in distant regions,*
> *Tell the Burmans Jesus died;*
> *Tell them Satan and his legions,*
> *Bow to him they crucified.*

Far beyond the mighty Ganges,
When vast floods beyond us roll,
Think how widely Jesus ranges
Nations wide from pole to pole.

Samuel and Harriet Newall were married almost immediately, as were Samuel and Roxana Nott. News of ships started coming in, and the young couples plus Luther Rice and Gordon Hall made their last-minute preparations for their voyage. Some were to go on one boat, the rest on another. Passages for the Newalls and Judsons were booked on *The Caravan*. But as well as human passengers - animals came too.

'Why are hens cooped up on deck?' Harriet asked her new husband.

'They'll provide eggs for the journey, and may even be eaten before the end of the voyage.'

Harriet pulled a face at the thought. Ann looked at the pigs being taken on board. 'Are they part of the larder too?' she asked.

'I should think so.' Adoniram smiled at his young wife. 'There's certainly going to be some fresh food provided!'

'It looks like a farmyard,' laughed Ann. 'There are the sacks of animal feed and there's the straw for bedding. All we need is a cow and a milkmaid.'

Harriet thought about that. 'They wouldn't be any good,' she decided. 'Cows would just fall over when the seas get rough.'

'You're quite right,' Ann agreed. 'We'll have eggs, poultry and pork, but no milk, butter, cheese or beef.'

'We'd better enjoy what meat we're given,' Adoniram reminded his friends. 'There will be little or none in a Buddhist country.'

'Of course!' Harriet remembered. 'Buddhists don't kill animals for food.'

Having unpacked in their tiny cabins, the two couples went on board to wave goodbye to their friends and supporters. But nothing happened. The boat didn't sail. Bad weather came in and the boat was held up for the next four days. Eventually the storm calmed and the pilot boat eased *The Caravan* out of port and into the open sea. In the light of an early dawn on 19th February 1812 the Judsons and Newalls watched America fade into the horizon. Each had their own thoughts about the years they had spent in their homeland, but they shared a dream of the life to come.

'We seem to be sitting lower in the water,' Samuel said, five days out of port.

'And there's a great flurry of activity below and hardly a sailor to be seen on deck,' added his wife.

The boat seemed to be listing to starboard. It was Ann who noticed that first.

'I think we should be praying,' she said urgently.

Then they realised, as she did, that the boat had sprung a leak and was in danger of sinking. Land was days away and not another ship was in sight. The sailors searched below for the leak. Four were lowered over the side to see if they could see from the way the vessel sat in the water where the hole was. For a while it was touch and go, but the sailors struggled on and the two young missionary couples prayed as they had rarely prayed before. And when the hole was found and repaired they were almost as tired as the sailors. They had been working just as hard.

1st May 1812,' Ann wrote in her diary. '*Today we crossed the equator. We've had many adventures since we left home, not all of them pleasant, but we're getting there. Somehow crossing the equator is a landmark (or should it be a seamark?) on our journey. And there is wonderful news to report. Harriet thinks she may be going to have a baby! She's hardly had time to be a wife now it seems she's to be a mother. I'm so thrilled for her, though it is an awesome thought to be having a first child in a strange land where the people don't speak our language.*

One hundred and fourteen days after leaving America, there was a shout from the top of the mast. 'Land ahoy! Land ahoy!'

Everyone rushed on deck to see India for the first time. Ann hugged her husband. Judson smiled back. All were looking forward to feeling dry land under their feet once more. But it was some days before the pilot boats came to take off *The Caravan's* passengers. Ann and Harriet remained on board while their husbands went ashore to register with the police.

'Where are you going?' the captain of the pilot boat asked Samuel.

He explained that they were to be in India for some time, but their final destination was Burma.

'That's a stupid idea!' the Indian retorted. 'Nobody in his right mind goes to Burma, especially not with two pretty women.' He had seen Ann and Harriet wave them off. The man held his arms out wide. 'That number of people are killed in Burma every year, even more.'

Neither of the missionaries took this too seriously, thinking their boatman was being alarmist. But when they met William Carey, an experienced English missionary, they discovered that his son was serving the Lord in Burma and that the man might have been telling the truth.

'We understood that there was only one missionary there - a Roman Catholic,' Judson said, thinking back to the books he had read.

Carey nodded. 'That was the case until Felix went, now he's the only missionary presence.' Seeing the hopeful look on Samuel and Adoniram's faces, Carey continued. 'I have to tell you this. Felix is only allowed to work in Burma because his wife is Burmese. In any case, it's not the kind of place you want to be, far less take your wives. Let me tell you just one story. Recently five hundred men who annoyed the king were buried alive. And that kind of thing is not uncommon.'

'But we can work here for a time,' Judson said, 'until things improve and the way is clear for us to go to Burma.'

Carey shook his head. 'The situation in Burma will not improve, and new missionaries are not welcome here either. I very much doubt that you'll get permission to stay.'

Although there was no dampening of their enthusiasm, it was with a little confusion that Adoniram and Samuel tried to explain the situation to their wives when they went to collect them off *The Caravan* and take them to meet William Carey. There was much discussion over the days that followed, and the outcome of it was that the old English missionary thought the young couples might find an area of service in either Mauritius or Madagascar. Plans were made in that direction. After some time in India, Samuel and Harriet left for Mauritius, with Adoniram and Ann to follow.

La Belle Creol

While the Judsons waited in Calcutta for a boat to Mauritius another ship arrived from America bringing their friends to join them.

'It will be wonderful to see them,' Ann enthused, as the landing formalities were gone through.

The newcomers were part of that little group which had prayed for God's work some years before. They were good friends of the Judsons, and there was a great deal of handshaking and hugging when they eventually met up. The plan had been for them to work together, but they decided to separate because Adoniram and Ann had become Baptists since leaving America. Luther Rice agreed to go along with the Judsons.

There was such a coming and going of confusion with the authorities that noises were made about sending Luther, Adoniram and Ann to England! This called for some quick thinking. The three of them boarded *La Belle Creol* for Mauritius and started on their way down the River Hooghly to the sea.

Ann soaked up the sights and sounds around them. She had never envisaged a river as wide as the Hooghly. Sea-going ships sailed up and down and it seemed that hundreds of little craft wove in and out between them as they went. At first she worried that there might be a collision, but she very soon realised that the boatmen were well used to the congestion.

'This river is like a vast shopping street,' she commented to her husband. 'Most of the little boats are laden with things to sell to the people on board the ships, and the others are like taxis waiting to take people off the boats to the shore.'

'And when they want to go on board again,' Luther explained, 'they take one of the ship-to-shore taxis and chase the ship up or downstream!'

Ann was fascinated by all that was going on around her, but the men had things on their minds.

'We're almost out of risk,' Luther said, as they sailed towards the mouth of the river.

Adoniram was tense. 'I'll not relax until we leave India behind us. The East India Company has the country in a stranglehold. What they say goes, and if they stop the ship and tell us to get off, that's exactly what we'll have to do. But for the time being I agree with you that things seem to be going well.'

'Look!' Ann said, pointing to a little boat which was edging into their wake. 'We're being followed.'

The two men were on their feet in a flash.

'It'll just be going to guide us through a difficult patch,' Luther told his friends.

Adoniram wasn't so sure. The pilot boat drew alongside and a man climbed aboard *La Belle Creol*.

'It'll be nothing to do with us,' Ann told her husband.

'Just you wait and see.'

Her two companions looked at each other. It was Adoniram who said what they were both thinking. 'We'll leave immediately on one of these small boats.' There were several weaving around their ship. 'You stay on board, Ann. They'll not bother about a woman. We'll send out a boat when it's dark to bring you and the luggage ashore. Meanwhile we'll find an inn where English is spoken. There seem to be plenty of them along the Hooghly.'

'I suppose they've learned the language over the years from English sailors.'

But Adoniram wasn't interested in what she was saying. He was still working out his plans.

'If the worst comes to the worst and we're not able to get you off you can go on to Mauritius and stay with Samuel and Harriet Newall until we arrive.'

With that they shimmied over the rail and jumped into a tiny rowing boat that had drawn in to pick them up and take them ashore.

'I have orders,' the pilot captain explained to the captain of *La Belle Creol*, 'to escort back to Calcutta those who are to be deported to England.'

'And who has given the orders?' he was asked.

'I've come on the authority of the East India Company.'

But the only one of the three missionaries that was left was Ann.

'My husband and Mr Rice are no longer aboard,' she

explained, when they found her.

The two captains looked across the wide river estuary. 'It's like searching for a needle in a haystack,' one said to the other. 'There must be dozens of small boats between here and the land.'

'I am required to inform you,' the pilot captain said in his most official voice, 'that you may not leave the River Hooghly for the sea with the missionaries on board.'

With that he turned on his heel, strode to the rail and was up, over and away in less time than it takes to tell.

That night Ann went by rowing-boat to the inn her husband had found, and the three agreed that they could hold up the boat no longer.

'I'm afraid that means you'll have to arrange to get the luggage off,' Adoniram told his wife. 'If we go back on board I'm liable to find myself in prison for the second time in my life. And that's not something I want to repeat.'

It was just as well they came to that conclusion because it was rather a stroppy captain who waited to help Ann back on board.

'I have no choice,' he said, 'but to ask you to take your things and leave. I have a job to do and I can't do it until you are clear of the boat.'

Ann thanked him. 'We do understand,' she assured him, 'and we've already decided to leave.'

The captain sighed with relief. 'I'll send two men to help you.'

But it wasn't quite as easy as it seemed as the only

small boats that were alongside couldn't take all the luggage. Ann had no need to explain the problem to the captain. He could see it for himself.

'I'll take you the sixteen miles down to the next inn and you'll be able to hire a bigger boat there. But that's my limit,' he insisted. 'It's more than my job's worth to take you any further. As it is, the rest of the passengers are complaining about the hold up.'

What luggage had been loaded on to the small boat was hauled off again, and all of this was done as *La Belle Creol* moved downriver. Despite all the hassle, Ann could not help but be impressed by the skill of the boatmen who seemed to be able to do the most complicated manoeuvres on the move!

'Do you think it's worth making one last attempt to get permission to stay?' Judson asked, as he and Rice discussed their desperate situation.

Luther thought about the options. 'Whether we go or stay we're at the mercy of the East India Company. They can prevent us from staying in India and they can stop a ship taking us away!'

'We've got to remember that however powerful they are, God is more powerful still.'

'You're right, Adoniram,' Luther said. 'It's so easy to get caught up in what's happening and to forget what's most important. Let's pray about what we should do.'

After the two men had prayed they discussed the situation once again and used the common sense God had given them. It was decided that Luther Rice should try one last time to get permission to stay in India, leaving his friend to cope with the tricky situation on the Hooghly. Adoniram rowed out to *La Belle Creol*. But as he rowed a breeze got up. The ship's captain took advantage of the wind, raised the anchor and sailed downriver. Adoniram's small boat hoisted its sail and set off in hot pursuit! When the ship reached the inn at which Ann was to get off, the Captain was unwilling to lose any time or wind so he only slowed down, he didn't drop anchor. By then Judson was some way behind. Ann jumped into a tiny boat and asked its owner to find her a boat big enough for the luggage. One was found and Ann boarded it and chased *La Belle Creol* which was sailing towards the sea with all their belongings. They caught up on the ship, went alongside, tied up, were carried along at the speed of the sailing ship and the luggage was offloaded as they moved. Ann watched it all happen, did what she could, and wondered if she was dreaming! When Adoniram arrived on his skiff, he discovered his wife overseeing the landing of their luggage at an inn on the bank of the river.

'Judson!' a voice called the following morning as they tried to work out how best to unload.

It was Luther Rice.

'What news?' Ann asked their friend.

Luther sat down on a sea chest and told them what had happened.

'God has been so good,' he said. 'I caught a boat almost immediately. And after I'd been to the East Indian

Company I was able to get one right back downriver again!'

Adoniram agreed that God had been good but he wanted to know the outcome of the exercise rather than the travel arrangements.

'We've been refused permission to stay,' Luther told the Judsons. 'But we've been given leave to go on *La Belle Creol* to Mauritius.'

Ann didn't know whether to laugh or cry. Adoniram was on his feet as though springs had sent him there.

'But it could be at sea by now in this wind,' he wailed.

'Where's the next place *La Belle Creol* will stop?' Luther asked the boatman.

The boat man thought for a minute. 'Saugur, and that's about seventy miles away.'

'Will you take us there with our luggage?' Luther and Adoniram asked in unison.

The man looked at them, looked at Ann, and looked at the luggage. Once he had negotiated a fair price all the missionaries got on board.

Adoniram and Luther took oars and pulled the boat into the channel while the boatman hoisted his sail to the wind. Fortunately the wind which had speeded the ship on its way was still blowing and the sail caught it right away. Despite lying low in the water because of the weight it was carrying, the boat fairly moved along. The three men took turns at the ropes so that no time was wasted because of tiredness. Ann, quite exhausted by all she had done, tried to rest.

'Will we catch up with the ship?' all four wondered. The three passengers prayed, knowing that God was more than able to move a small boat more quickly than a ship. And the fourth, the boatman, waited and watched in amusement to see what these crazy people would do next! When they got to Saugur *La Belle Creol* was still there, though the captain may not have been best pleased to see them. The Judsons and Luther Rice praised God, and the boatman laughed, shrugged his shoulders, then helped them reload their luggage.

Seven weeks later, on 17th January 1813, *La Belle Creol* sailed into harbour in Mauritius.

'I'll be so glad to stand on solid ground again,' Ann told her husband. 'Now I understand how Harriet felt. Being pregnant and sailing don't go together as I've now discovered for myself.'

Adoniram smiled down at her. The thought of being parents thrilled them both. Ann longed to hear news of her friend, Harriet, knowing that she must by then have had her baby. But the worst of news awaited them when they landed.

'Dead?' Ann said, in a tiny voice that could hardly be heard. 'Both Harriet and the baby are dead?'

She couldn't cry. Her pain was too great to be released in tears.

'Harriet was just nineteen,' she whispered to herself. 'She was hardly more than a child herself.'

Ann's heart was so sore, but it was nothing to the grief Samuel Newall felt. He and Harriet had been so full of plans, so full of anticipation and excitement. Now he was alone, a childless father, a widower. His world had fallen apart.

The new missionaries worked in Mauritius for some months, but the situation there made them feel that it wasn't where God wanted them to be. They gathered together to discuss the future.

'The time has come to make a decision,' Adoniram said to his companions. 'Tell me all your thinking.'

Luther Rice, who had been really quite ill over their short time in Mauritius, told them he wanted to go back to America to start a Baptist mission organisation there, one that would support the kind of work the others were doing.

'I've decided to go to Bombay to work there,' Samuel Newall told them. 'I can't stay here.'

Everyone understood.

'And I think we should go to Madras and see where the Lord leads us from there,' Judson said.

Ann nodded her head in agreement.

In Madras an extraordinary thing happened - they found that a boat was about to leave for Rangoon. And Rangoon is in Burma! Despite advice from every side telling them not to go, the Judsons arranged their passage, saw their luggage stowed on board, then climbed up the gangway themselves. They were going to Burma at last! But tragedy struck before they arrived. Ann went into labour and their child was born dead and buried at sea.

After a further three weeks at sea, on 13th July 1813, Adoniram and Ann Judson reached Rangoon.

'Look at that!' Adoniram said, pointing to the Shwe Dagon Pagoda. 'The captain tells me that the spire is recovered in pure gold every four years!'

Ann looked at the sight, but her heart felt dead inside her. Adoniram tried to interest her in all the things they were passing - the thatched bamboo and teak houses along the river bank, the muddy creeks and the fort-like enclosure in the centre of Rangoon. But his wife was too sad, too ill and too exhausted to take notice.

Early days

As Ann was carried ashore on a chair she held her head down. She wasn't well enough to take notice of her surroundings. Her heart was back at sea with her lost baby, and she had no energy or interest for anything else. Although she didn't raise her head to look around her she couldn't help but be aware of the noises of the place - the tinkling and clanking of pagoda bells, the squeals and laughter of children at play, and the chatter of the bustling little town of Rangoon. But it all seemed to be happening at a distance. In her sorrow and heartbreak, Ann felt utterly alone.

'Who is that hiding her face under such a funny hat?' a Burmese woman asked her friend.

'Let's go and see.'

The two women went right up to the chair Ann was being carried on, stooped down and peered under her bonnet, totally unembarrassed as they did so. Ann, still with eyes cast down, looked into the smiling faces and sparkling eyes of the two women. Despite herself she smiled back, raised her head, and discovered that she was surrounded by a crowd of people, mainly women, who burst out laughing with delight when they saw her face. The warm glow Ann felt in her heart surprised her.

'Who are you?'

'What are you doing here?'

'Where are you staying?'

'How long are you in Rangoon for?'

Questions came from every side, but all were in Burmese. Although the new missionaries realised a kindly interest was being taken in them, they had no idea what was being said.

My first impressions of Rangoon, Adoniram wrote to his sister, Abigail, within a short time of arriving. *The first thing you notice here is the noise. There's a lot of laughter. The Burmese are happy by nature despite the terrible things that happen here. And the pagodas generate more noise than you could imagine. Little bells tinkle and bigger bells dong and often they do it all together. It's like being in a percussion band practice! And children, who seem to be everywhere, shout and sing and whistle and laugh as they play.*

Then there are the colours. At home in America - oh dear, I mustn't say that any longer because Burma is home - people wear such dark colours, black and brown and deep blue with only a dash of brightness in a scarf or necktie. It's so different here. Even the men wear vivid colours, and because the sun shines so brightly the market place looks like a flower garden! She felt so out of place in her sober clothing that she changed to wearing lighter things, though we've some way to go before we catch up with the rest of the population of Rangoon. You'd hardly recognise your sister-in-law if you saw her in the street!

And the next thing you notice are the smells. Believe it or not the most pervading smell is of tobacco. Men and women, even

*children and babies smoke thick cigars. When Ann saw a child
less than a year old smoking she actually squealed, thinking
the little girl had picked up the lit cigar and would be burned.
However, just a quick look around showed us that children are
given lit cigars to smoke. They seem to use them as comforters
in the way I used my striped blanket as a comforter when I was
a child. Do you still have it, by the way?*

As the weeks passed Ann felt more like her old
self, and she began to enjoy being out and about in
Rangoon.

'Have you ever seen such bright colours?' she asked
Adoniram as they took a short walk together. 'The
women are like butterflies. They look so comfortable
and I feel out of place even in the white dress I had made
for me. Do you think I could wear Burmese dress?' she
asked.

Adoniram thought about it. 'We certainly stick out
like sore thumbs dressed as we are. I believe that it would
help us to be accepted if you wore what everyone else
wears. And you'd look so pretty in an embroidered top
and a brightly coloured silk skirt.'

'I love the way the skirts are gathered up and tucked
into neat folds at the top, and how elegantly their red
embroidered borders hang. The light silk shawls are very
pretty too,' his wife added, 'they look like butterflies
wings.'

Adoniram looked into her hazel eyes. 'Will you wear
a flower in your hair like all the other women?'

Ann smiled. 'If I'm going to dress as they do I might

Danger on the Streets of Gold

feel unfinished without my hair tied up in a knot and finished with a flower!'

They walked on in silence for a while.

'Will you wear Burmese dress if I do?' Ann asked.

Her husband looked at the men as they passed. Each wore a pasto, a loose white vest tied with strings that hung loose. And instead of trousers they wrapped about 7 metres of soft coloured silk around themselves, then knotted it up in front of each leg. It was certainly very different!

'I'll think about that,' he said 'though I refuse to have myself covered in the blue tattoos that seem to be part of the fashion here.'

Ann smiled. 'They're not quite you, are they?'

And as they walked back to the mission house, Ann Judson tried to picture her husband tattooed like the men they were passing, with swirling patterns, leaves, birds and animals on every area of bare skin. But it was too much for her mind to take in!

'I'm becoming quite used to the food here,' Adoniram said one lunchtime, after they had given thanks for their second rice meal of the day.

'Don't you miss pork and beef and mutton?' Ann asked.

Her husband shrugged. 'There's no point in missing it,' he said, 'because we're not going to get it as long as we are in Burma. Buddhists see all life as sacred and won't slaughter any for food.'

'It bothers me that they eat animals that have died

naturally though. They might have died of diseases that pass on to those who eat them,' Ann thought aloud.

'But what I don't understand,' Judson said, 'is why hens are sometimes available.'

'That has puzzled me too! And who could have thought that we'd soon develop a taste for rice and more rice and curried rice and more rice, and rice with cucumber for a change!'

Adoniram grinned at the thought then his face grew serious. 'There is so much poverty here that we should feel thankful for whatever we have, and however little of it we have.'

Having agreed to keep a mission report for the churches in America, Adoniram settled down one afternoon to compose his early impressions of Burma.

The country presents a rich, beautiful appearance,' he wrote, '*everywhere is covered with vegetation, and if cultivated, it would be one of the finest in the world. But the poor natives have no inducement to labour or raise anything, as it would probably be taken from them by their oppressive rulers. Many of them live on leaves and vegetables that grow spontaneously, and some actually die of hunger. Everything is extremely costly, therefore many are induced to steal whatever comes their way. There are constant robberies and murders committed; scarcely a night passes that a house is not broken open and things stolen.*

It was a serious Adoniram Judson who laid down

his quill pen. For a few minutes he felt oppressed at the prospect of the society his young wife would have to live in, but then a wave of relief flooded through him. 'God called us here,' he thought. 'And he is here with us. What better company could we have!'

Adoniram wasn't the only one to put his new experiences into writing. *There is so much beauty here,* Ann confided to her diary, *but there are things that would make me squirm if I allowed them to. On the one hand, the women are dressed like garden flowers, on the other, they chew something called betel until their mouths drip scarlet like blood and their teeth turn black. And the children are pretty as can be, but they go around with cigars in their mouths! Women and girls are bedecked with jewellery, but the men and boys wear strings to protect them from evil spirits. And the children! They wear not a stitch of clothing, just bracelets, anklets, necklaces and spirit strings! It makes me unspeakably sad to think that these dear people believe that a piece of dirty string can protect them from evil when all the while our lovely and loving Lord Jesus is holding out his arms to welcome them to the eternal safety of his love.*

'Your Burmese is coming on well,' Felix Carey told the Judsons, when he visited them in Rangoon. 'You're both gifted in languages.'

Adoniram laughed. 'When I first saw written Burmese I wondered if I'd ever be able to read or write it. It looks like a series of circles and parts of circles written in an never-ending line!'

Felix grinned. 'I know what you mean. That's because

there are no sentences, no paragraphs, and there's no punctuation.'

'It doesn't help that it's written on banana leaves!' Ann added. 'It makes the writing even more difficult to read.'

'You are better at speaking the language than Adoniram is,' Felix said. 'But his reading and writing are splendid.'

'Do you think we speak well enough to visit Mya-day-men?' asked Judson.

Carey thought for a minute. 'It's important that you meet the city governor as soon as you're able, and I think that time has come.'

Arrangements were made for Adoniram to visit Mya-day-men and for Ann to visit his main wife. Her visit was more successful than his. A white woman was a novelty, especially one who wore Burmese dress. But when Judson visited the governor the man hardly looked at him.

'He didn't seem interested in me at all,' he commented to Felix, on returning from the visit.

'That's typical,' his friend assured him. 'Just be encouraged that he agreed to see you and that he didn't keep you waiting for hours. That kind of thing matters here.'

Adoniram was still considering this when Felix broke into his thoughts. 'I've been offered a government job,' he said, 'and I feel inclined to take it. I'd like to go back to India to discuss it with my father. Would you be happy for my wife and son to stay with you while I'm away?'

Judson's brain went into overdrive. 'That would make me the only male missionary in the country,' he thought. But aloud he assured Felix that his family was welcome to stay, though he would rather they all moved out of the mission house.

And it was as well that they did. In January 1814, shortly after they moved, there was a violent robbery at the next but one building to the mission house. God cared for his servants in Burma. One Sunday while Felix was still in India, the Judsons and Mrs Carey went with her little son to the mission house for the day. While they were there, a fire broke out in Rangoon and nearly all the town was burned down.

When Felix returned from India, it was with the news that he had decided to take the job and to move to the city of Ava. The journey was by river-boat, and en route to Ava the boat overturned and Mrs Carey and their little boy were drowned.

Ann and Adoniram mourned the loss of their friend and her son. The life of a missionary was a hard and difficult one. The land of Burma was beautiful, but with the heartache they had already suffered, they also knew it could be cruel.

'Do you think we are making the best use of our time?' Adoniram asked his wife, after some months living on their own in Rangoon.

'I think so,' she assured him. 'You're making progress

with the written language. You've started to compile a word list from which to make up a dictionary, you're working on a book of Burmese grammar, and your translation of Matthew's gospel is coming on well.'

'It's very slow work,' her husband said. 'There's just a little progress each day.'

'It has to be slow to be thorough,' Ann reminded him. 'There's no point in rushing any of these jobs and making mistakes in them. Imagine if you got the grammar book or dictionary wrong. A future missionary here might find himself asking for a beating with the rudder rather than a meeting with the ruler!'

Judson laughed. 'You're quite right. It's better to be slow and accurate than to have the next generation beaten with rudders!'

Early in 1815 Ann became ill and didn't seem to be recovering. It was decided that she should go to Madras for medical care and a rest. When she came back six weeks later she was much better.

'A letter has come from America!' Ann said excitedly, as she rushed with it into her husband's tiny study soon after her return. She sat down beside him to hear what it said. And she was glad to sit down, as the baby she was carrying was due in just a day or two.

'It's from Luther Rice,' Adoniram told her as he scanned the letter. 'And listen to this, "There are now Baptist Missionary Societies in nearly every state and they are all fund-raising for the work."'

'That is good news. What else does he say?'

'It seems that there's a new missionary on his way out right now! He's called George Hough and he's a printer. Luther says that he'll be able to print the Bible in Burmese as we translate it because he's bringing a printing press with him! And here's something that will thrill you ... Hough is married and he's bringing his wife, Phoebe, with him!'

Ann's face glowed with pleasure. 'God is so good,' she said 'so good.'

Just six days after that letter arrived, on 11th September 1815, little Roger Judson was born, much to the delight and thankfulness of his parents. And when Roger was three weeks old the Judsons' language teacher expressed an interest in the gospel, the first Burmese person to do so.

'This is delightful,' Ann often told her husband in the weeks and months that followed. 'Here we are together, studying the language which our son will grow up speaking naturally. And he's lying on the floor between us gurgling in what could be either Burmese or English, who can tell!'

But that happy time came to an end the following spring. Roger stopped gaining weight. He stopped his happy gurgling. He stopped kicking his little legs in the air. And one day he stopped breathing. Roger Judson, the darling son of Adoniram and Ann, was dead.

The governor's wife was really upset. She was fond of Ann and she'd been enchanted by the little white baby. By way of comforting her grieving friends she arranged a picnic a few days after Roger's death and invited them to join her. The custom there meant they could not refuse the invitation, though a picnic was the last thing they wanted to go to. When an elephant arrived for them the Judsons realised it was going to be a grand affair, but it was beyond their wildest imaginings. Thirty men with guns and spears led the parade, then came two elephants. Adoniram and Ann were helped into a howdah on one of them, their hostess was on the other. Several other elephants followed bearing the governor's son and a number of government officials. Between two and three hundred young women brought up the rear. The procession took them through three miles of dense jungle to the governor's beautiful garden where they had their picnic. It was all very colourful, all very beautiful. But Adoniram and Ann could not help but compare that splendid garden with the one at the mission house, the one in which their dear little son was buried.

Goings and comings

'I think some exercise would do you good,' an English sea captain told Adoniram a month or two after Roger's death. 'It would help clear up these headaches of yours.'

The man, a Christian, was staying with the Judsons for a while. Arrangements were made to acquire horses, and the two took to riding first thing each morning.

'Your wife is doing a splendid job with her school,' the captain told Adoniram one day as they rode. 'She was telling me that she has between twenty and thirty pupils coming regularly. And she's nearly finished her book of questions and answers about Christianity. That will be a great help in the work.'

'It certainly will. She has really thrown herself into the mission since Roger died. And when she's not teaching or writing or studying, she's out talking to the women and telling them about the Lord Jesus. That's where her book will be useful. We'll be able to give it to anyone we meet who shows an interest in the faith.'

'It's a great pity that the Hough family have been held up. The sooner the printing press is here the better. Have you any idea when they and it might come?'

Judson shrugged his shoulders. 'It looks as though it

won't be before the autumn. But although the delay is holding up printing, the translation work can go on.'

'And so it does,' laughed the captain. And I imagine that it's those long hours translating that caused your headaches. Are they really getting better, by the way?'

'They are indeed. I'm sure your insistence that we ride each day has done the trick. And I enjoy it too.'

'So do I.'

December 1816.

   Dear Abigail,

   You'll be delighted to learn that the Houghs finally arrived about six weeks ago! The printing press is set up and we are making preparation to print a seven page leaflet outlining Christianity and explaining about the work we are doing. We'll print a thousand copies of that. We're also planning to print Ann's book of questions and answers. It's exciting to see things moving forward. You have no idea how much the gospel is needed in Burma. There is such beauty and such violence here. You'll find it hard to believe, but executions are so common they are seen as a form of community entertainment, and disembowelment is a regular form of punishment here. Please remember us in your prayers, as I know you do.

   Your loving brother, Adoniram

'I think you should go,' Ann encouraged her husband in May the following year. 'If there are Christians just over the border into Bengal, it would be good for you to meet up with them. And you won't be away for too long. Even if you are delayed, the Houghs are here in Rangoon. It's not as though I'm being left alone.'

'I'm still in two minds. There seems to be so much to do here too. Think of it. I've only translated five chapters of Matthew's gospel. But I do agree that it would be good if I met them.'

'You can take Matthew with you,' Ann pointed out. 'The translation work needn't stop because you're travelling.'

'I wonder what has happened to the man who was here about six weeks ago, the one who took a copy of everything Hough has printed so far. We've not heard that he's become a believer, but there are rumours that he's showing the printed pages to all his friends. We'll have to keep praying for him.'

Ann smiled. 'That's something else you can do as you travel.'

Her husband grinned. 'You're a hard task master. Here I was looking for a nice relaxing holiday!'

It took some time to make preparation for the journey. Adoniram had to find out exactly where the Christians were and how to get to them. He also wrote a letter to them which he hoped would arrive before he did. Then a boat had to be found, provisions taken for the journey, and work arranged that could be done en route. Eventually the time came to leave, and Adoniram did so with the promise that he would write to his wife regularly.

* * *

Months passed with no word from Judson. At first Ann thought that mail was going missing, then she wondered if he was ill. Hough, who was quite a pessimist, decided that Adoniram had died! But the missionaries were not the only ones who had worries because Rangoon was hit by cholera.

'What on earth is that noise?' Phoebe Hough asked, her hands held over her ears.

'You'll have to get used to it because it could go on for days.'

'I can't take much more of this,' Phoebe wept. 'It's driving me into a nervous wreck. But what is it anyway?'

'Because the people think cholera is caused by evil spirits they make as much noise as they can to frighten them away. If you go into the town you'll discover they're all beating the wooden walls of their houses with whatever is available.'

A shudder went through Phoebe Hough. 'I won't do that. I could get cholera or be caught up in the frenzy out there. I might even be killed.' There was a note of hysteria in her voice. 'And Adoniram isn't here to help when he's needed.'

Ann put her arms round her friend. 'No,' she agreed. 'But God is. And all the noise in the world won't scare the Lord away.'

The young woman finally began to relax.

'It's just that everything is going wrong at the same

time,' Phoebe said, by way of explaining her outburst. 'What with cholera, the possibility of war between England and Burma, and that business of George too. That really unnerved me.'

Ann was sympathetic. 'I know George was detained by the authorities. And I know the questioning was ferocious. But he wasn't actually assaulted in any way. And when I wrote to the city governor his captors were quick to free him.'

'I know,' Phoebe agreed. 'But I can't help thinking what might have happened.'

As sympathy wasn't helping, Ann's voice took on a firmer tone. 'But it didn't happen and let's be grateful for that. Now, if you'll excuse me, I must get back to work.'

When she was alone Ann Judson did some serious thinking. She could understand her friend's fears because Rangoon was a dangerous place to be from many points of view. It was not a very law-abiding town. Theft and assaults were commonplace. The authorities were unpredictable, sometimes seeming happy to let the missionaries do their work, then overnight becoming opposed to it. And opposition could come in the form of awkwardness, detainment and questioning, and … well, she didn't want to think about that.

Ann gave herself a shake. 'That's all very well,' she thought. 'Those are legitimate reasons for feeling fearful. But God is right here in this situation with us and that's all I need to know. In any case, what have I to fear compared with these poor Burmese people who live in daily fear of evil spirits, never being sure that they won't be attacked by a spirit of illness, or a spirit of death, or a spirit of a thousand and one other disasters. Gracious me, Ann Judson!' she said to herself. 'They have good cause to be afraid. And I'll be of little or no use to them if I'm fearful too.'

Ann's talking-to stood her in good stead because she was about to go through a difficult time, many months without word from her husband. When, nearly a year after leaving, Judson had not returned, the Houghs decided that they could take no more, that they would go to India and do the printing there. Ann was prevailed upon to join them, though she left much against her will. Still believing that her husband was alive, she persuaded their language teacher to go with them in case they should meet up again. At the last minute the man changed his mind and jumped ashore.

'Dear Lord,' Ann prayed, as the boat pulled into the channel for the start of its trip downriver. Show me if I'm doing the right thing. I pray that you will give me peace if I'm meant to remain on the boat, and a restless spirit if I should leave.'

Ann lay down on her narrow berth and did not sleep at all. The same happened the following night, and the next night again. She tossed and turned and didn't get a wink of sleep.

'Thank you, Lord,' she prayed, when she got up, exhausted by sleepless nights. 'You've certainly given me a restless spirit. And thank you that you know the way I should go, and that you've shown it to me. Now, Heavenly Father, please give me an opportunity to get off this boat before I find myself on the ocean.'

At the mouth of the river, just before heading for the open sea, the ship listed to one side. The cargo in the hold had slipped and the boat was in danger of sinking. It went into port to redistribute the weight of the cargo, and while it was there Ann disembarked and went back to Rangoon, deciding that was where she should remain and that was where her husband would look for her when (she never thought 'if') he returned. Soon after she got home she heard that Adoniram was alive. Ten days later the Houghs returned, their sailing having been delayed by several weeks. Within days another boat arrived in Rangoon. Adoniram Judson was on board! God had led Ann back just on time to welcome him home.

It took some days for the Judsons to catch up with each other and for him to tell of his journey. Having discovered that his ship was a crate and the captain a drunkard, he explained, he had disembarked and gone overland to Madras. That was why he had been away so long, though neither ever found out why his letters home didn't arrive. Ann was full of news too: what had been happening in Rangoon, the cholera and its terrible consequences, and the Houghs' ups and downs. Both had a mixed bag of news, but the seriousness of much of what they had to say to each other was almost lost in their delight at being together again.

* * *

Shortly after Adoniram's return to Rangoon two more American missionary couples arrived to join them. Sadly both men caught tuberculosis soon after arriving. That was the last straw for the Houghs. They moved the printing operation to Calcutta in India. With all these comings and goings it seemed to Adoniram a good time to look at the whole mission strategy.

'The problem is that the mission house is not right in the town,' Judson said to his new colleagues.

'We can't change where it is.'

But we could build a zayat on pagoda street.'

'A zayat?'

Adoniram explained his thinking. 'The priests live in the pagodas, only coming out in their saffron robes and with their begging bowls. It's so sad that people think they can earn favour with their gods by giving the priests money. Buddhists who aren't priests don't usually go to pagodas, they go to zayats. I think one of the reasons people don't come here is that they see us as priests and think the mission house, like a pagoda, is not for ordinary people like them. If we were to build a zayat I believe they would feel freer to come.'

The decision was made and the work began. For a month the Judsons oversaw the building work. Theirs' was not ornate like a Buddhist zayat, but dignified and plain.

27th June, 1819,

Dear Papa, when I last wrote we were just about to start building. What a lot has happened since then. We held our first service in the zayat on 4th April and several people we'd not seen before came to see what we were about! A stream of people have come through the door since then, and we've had many good conversations about the Lord. It helped that Adoniram and I went to a Buddhist service to see what it was like. Now we understand the people a little better, and they seem to realise that.

On the last day of April a poor man came to the zayat. He is about thirty five years old. His name is Maung Nau. He was very attentive, and he came back to our Sunday service. The next day, and the next again, he spent hours talking to Adoniram. At a meeting on 5th May it seemed he was near to becoming a Christian … and the following Sunday he professed faith in Jesus! Maung Nau is our very first convert. Papa, after nearly six years in Burma we have a convert - and that makes it all worthwhile! We had a problem right away as Maung Nau had been offered a job in Ava and we didn't want to lose him. So Adoniram has given him work here. Today we had the great thrill of seeing him baptised.

The baptism service was delayed because King Bodawpaya died and his grandson King Bagyidaw was enthroned in his place. Our joy at Maung Nau's conversion could so easily have been lost in what happened then. In order to ensue a long, peaceful and serene reign, King Bagyidaw had fourteen hundred members of the middle class and royal family put to death! It was against that background that over thirty of us gathered in the zayat today for a service after which we went to a pond nearby

*at the side of which is a large statue of Buddha, and there our
dear Maung Nau was baptised. There are tears in my eyes as I
write, tears of sorrow for the horrors of this past week, and tears
of joy that a Burmese brother has been saved.*

Your loving daughter, Ann.

*Ps. I've told you before about the two other Westerners in Rangoon,
Gibson and Rogers, who both have Burmese nationality and work
for the royal court. They're not interested in the faith at all, but
they are interested to see what becomes of Maung Nau.*

One of the two new American missionary couples left
Rangoon. He was not recovering from tuberculosis,
and Burma was not the place for him. He died shortly
afterwards. Having been gifted with an ability to learn
languages, Ann studied Siamese and, when she was
competent enough, she translated her book of questions
and answers and other material into Siamese. But the
Judsons' heads were not just stuck in books, they were
very much people people.

'The brother and sister from pagoda street have asked
if they can build a shack in the mission house grounds,'
Adoniram told his wife in the summer of 1819. 'How
many more can we take?'

Ann grinned. 'I'm still not used to the Burmese
custom of building a shack wherever you want to be,
even if it's in someone else's garden!'

'The sister has such a furious temper, I wonder how
she'll get on with the others.'

'The Lord is coping with her temper, Adoniram. I

think he's doing great things in her life.'

'And the others will be given grace to cope with her outbursts. Maung Ing especially shows real signs of faith.'

'It's interesting,' Ann said. 'When Jesus was alive it was poor people who were interested in his teaching, with only one or two well-educated and wealthy people like Nicodemus paying attention to him. That's just the same with us. All our enquirers are poor apart from the teacher.'

'He and I have such interesting discussions. I pray he'll come to faith in Jesus.'

On 7th November 1819, two of the men who lived in their garden were baptised as the sun set. But soon afterwards there was an upsurge of Buddhism under the new King Bagyidaw and the numbers attending the zayat dropped. The missionaries decided to try to get an audience with the king, or as the Burmese put it, to bow at the Golden Feet and lift their eyes to the Golden Face. And they hoped for some support from Gibson and Rogers who were in Ava, the western contacts at the king's court.

The Golden Presence

Ann watched the preparations for her husband's journey to Ava, where the king's court was located. Eighteen oarsmen were hired along with a steersman who, for the 350 miles of the trip to the capital city, would sit under the shade of a big umbrella and direct operations from there. A government representative arranged to travel with them, and two cooks and a Hindu washerman, along with one or two others made up the crew and passenger list of the river boat.

Adoniram took notes as he travelled. *The Irrawaddy is a vast river, and over the centuries many cities have been built along its length. Most of them are now abandoned and derelict. Successive kings have built their own cities, and the population has followed the court into them leaving their previous homes to decay. We have an Englishman on board who has been unfortunate all his life and now wishes to try the service of the Burman majesty. It is not for me to advise him about a possible career, but from all accounts that is not a job I should want to have. People fall out of favour here just as cities do, and they are cast aside - not always with their heads still on their shoulders. I'll tell this poor man as much as he's prepared to listen to, but he has a mind of his own, and not a very sound one. That probably explains why he's in the desperate state he's in. I shall call him John Smith in case anything happens to me and this diary is found and read.*

'He's got an easy job,' Smith commented to Adoniram, indicating with his head that the comment was about the steersman.

Judson turned round. The man looked as though he was on a river holiday. He was half sitting, halfflying under his umbrella, and his eyes seemed only halfopen. But the missionary knew better.

'He has to have his wits about him though,' he assured the Englishman. 'And the further up the Irrawaddy we go, the more you'll be aware of it.'

Smith was not convinced. 'If ever there was an easy job that's it ... check for rocks to the side and keep an eye open for rapids in front.'

Adoniram looked at the wide river and wondered where his companion expected to find rapids for the next hundred miles, or rocks for that matter!

'I suppose he's thinking of an English river,' the missionary thought and smiled.

Two weeks later they were still en route up the river, but it was narrower now, and even Smith was becoming aware of its dangers.

'I don't feel comfortable when we go ashore to buy food,' he said. 'The people are not exactly friendly.'

'The further upriver we go, the more that's true,' Judson told him very quietly. 'Eventually it will become unwise for us to get off at all.'

The missionary opened his books and continued

with his translation work. The last thing he wanted to do was to criticise the Burmese people. It could be that some of the oarsmen had worked on seagoing ships and had learned a little English. And if that were the case and Judson was heard making unwise statements, he might find himself floating down the Irrawaddy towards Rangoon, dead. John Smith took the hint, and when they did speak it was about what they were seeing around them.

One morning the Englishman burst out laughing. 'Look at that!' He pointed to the trees at the side of the ever narrowing river. 'They're having a grand old time.'

Adoniram followed the direction of his gaze and smiled. 'Monkeys are a perfect nuisance,' he told his travelling companion, 'but they are good for entertainment. And they are clever little blighters, thieves and robbers though they are.'

'What do you mean?'

'If you were ashore there you'd soon find out. Leave something on the ground and turn your back and they're off with it. The first you'll know is a squabble between them as they argue about who can have it and what it is for!'

Smith laughed heartily.

'One of the most entertaining sights I've seen here was a family of monkeys who had stolen a wide-brimmed hat experimenting with what they could use it for. It was on every part of them, thrown between them, hung on branches, filled with stones. One of them put it on his head, and at such a cheeky angle that even the owner of the hat was entertained.'

'Did he get it back?'

'No. The last time he saw it was when a young monkey took it high into a tree and two older ones set off in pursuit.'

Smith sighed happily. 'That's done me good,' he said. 'This long journey is getting me down. We've been on the Irrawaddy for three weeks now and the steersman says we've still more than a week to go.'

Two days later the boat was pursued by a pirate craft. Adoniram's crew was tired from their long journey, and they knew they had nothing to lose, so they put on very little speed in an effort to escape it. Smith lashed out when the pirates boarded, and he came off worse. Two black eyes, several other cuts and bruises plus a thorough soaking in the Irrawaddy was all he gained for his punches, and he lost most of his luggage too. Adoniram, who surprised the pirates with his ability to speak Burmese, prayed as the boat was searched. And his perch for praying was a bundle roughly wrapped in brown cloth, especially packed like that by Ann to avoid attention at such a time as this. When the pirates eventually jumped back on to their boat, Adoniram's prayers for the safety of his luggage turned to a song of thanks to God. His bundle was still intact. He still had his gift for King Bagyidaw.

On 25th January 1820, the crew raised their oars for

the last time on that journey, and the steersman jumped ashore and tied the boat securely to a tree.

'How far is it to Ava from here?' Smith asked.

Adoniram told him it was just a few miles.

'What are you going to do?'

'I'm going to find Mya-day-men. He was the Governor of Rangoon for a time and we got to know him well. He may be able to arrange for me to get into the Golden Presence.'

'Would he be able to get me a job?' enquired Smith.

'No, you couldn't ask someone as high powered as him. But I'll introduce you to two Englishmen who may be able to help you.'

On his way to see Mya-day-men Adoniram took John Smith to meet Gibson and Rogers, and left him with them.

Mya-day-men and his wife welcomed Adoniram. They asked kindly for Ann, and were disappointed to learn that there were still no Judson babies. Since the picnic she organised for them after little Roger died, Mya-day-men's wife had felt deeply their lack of children.

'Our freedom to speak about God is being severely curtailed,' Adoniram told Mya-day-men after they went through their ceremonial greetings. 'It's not that we're being persecuted, but the people who want to listen to us are, and those who come to our zayat are often taken into custody and questioned, sometimes forcefully.'

While his Burmese friend was a convinced Buddhist, he was still willing to argue for freedom of religion.

'So what are you hoping to achieve from an audience with the Golden Presence?'

'I want to ask for sufficient freedom of belief so that those who want to learn more about the Lord Jesus should be able to come to us without fear of the consequences.'

The Burman stood, the sign that it was time Judson left.

'I'll see what I can do for you. But I can make no promises.'

Adoniram had only been back at the boat for a few hours when a messenger came from Mya-day-men that Judson had to go to the Golden Throne the following day.

The missionary, who had prayed for this as he walked back from Ava to the boat, nearly jumped with excitement at the speed of the answer to his prayer. The boatmen, who were relaxing at the riverside, looked at him and grinned to each other. Their expressions said that they thought the American was mad. The messenger had told them that their passenger had been called into the Golden Presence, and they reckoned that his joy was misplaced, for they doubted that he'd come out alive. The only thing that worried them was that they might not be paid. Judson, who knew what they were saying and understood their concern, paid the steersman for the trip to Ava, and made him promise to wait for the return journey.

At dawn the next day Adoniram unwrapped his precious bundle, exposing a six-volume Bible covered in pure gold leaf.

'Will King Bagyidaw think this is a suitable gift?' he wondered. 'He would if he could see it for what it really is, the Word of the King of Kings and Lord of Lords. And if he recognised its worth he'd not mind if it was covered with brown paper rather than gold leaf.'

Praying fervently as they went, Adoniram and a companion arrived at the Golden Palace a few hours later. They were taken through golden halls with tall golden pillars. Everything they passed was covered in gold. The glow from it was like that of mellow sunshine.

'This Bible is going to seem a puny gift to the king,' Judson thought as he surveyed the tons of gold all around him. 'If only he could see it for the treasure it really is.'

A golden double door swung open before them and they processed into a golden hall even more beautiful than those they'd gone through before. The gold that covered the pillars was worked with amazingly intricate patterns and sunlight danced on the golden floor. There was a feeling of awe and expectancy all around them as gorgeously-dressed officials moved slowly and gracefully about their business.

Suddenly there was a sound like a thousand butterflies flapping their wings. Adoniram and his companion watched as every Burman in the hall fell to the floor, their silk clothes fluttering down behind them. Judson and his companion knelt, folding their hands respectfully.

'Who are these?' asked the Golden Voice.

'What happened then?' Ann asked, when her husband returned to Rangoon weeks later.

Adoniram's face looked sad at the memory. 'Well he wasn't in the least impressed with our gift,' he began. 'And he was even less impressed with our request. Far from agreeing to allow a degree of religious freedom, he announced the appointment of a hundred new Buddhist priests the very next day. It was a totally wasted journey.'

Ann tried to be encouraging. 'There's a Bible now inside the Golden Palace. Who knows what God can do through it if someone should read it in years to come.'

Judson looked at his wife. 'God is so good,' he thought, as he watched her rise and pour more tea. 'He has given me a wife like no other. She has supported me in ways I could never have imagined. She doesn't complain about my long and frequent absences and she's always positive even when things discourage me. I've so much to be thankful for.'

'And what's been happening here?' Adoniram asked, when he had poured out the last of his Ava story.

Ann smiled. 'Our three dear converts are growing bolder by the day. Although they remain very discreet they are always talking about Jesus.'

'Despite the fact they know what might happen to them?'

'That's right. And that should be a real encouragement to us. God can work through them just as easily as he can work through the Golden Presence.'

For the first time since his return, Judson relaxed.

'Thank you so much for reminding me of that. It's so easy to get into the mindset that thinks that the rich are more important than the poor when, in terms of Christianity, the opposite is so often the case.'

Ann thought of the three converts, poor men all, and smiled at the prospect of what God could do through them.

Before long there were two more conversions. In spite of the persecution, Burmans were believing in Jesus!

'Do you think the teacher will believe one day?' Ann asked. 'He's been coming here for so long with his deep and thought-provoking questions.'

'Not only that, he's started sending other people who are showing an interest too.'

'Because of his high position his very life would be in danger if he professed faith in Jesus.'

'I know that. I'm sure it's fear that's holding him back, fear for himself and for his family too.'

'We'll just have to keep praying.'

And they did.

A room in the mission house was set aside as a zayat and the old zayat was abandoned. It was no longer a good idea to meet right in the middle of pagoda street.

'I'm sorry we're going to have to leave, at least for a time,' Adoniram told the believers at a meeting in the summer of 1820. 'But you know my eyesight is causing problems, especially in the translation work, and the nearest place I can get treatment is Bengal.'

There was a knock at Judson's study door a few days after he heard the news. It was the teacher.

'I have trusted in the Lord Jesus,' he told the missionary. 'And I wish to apply to be baptised before you leave for Bengal.'

Adoniram's eyes filled with tears of happiness.

'How did you come to faith?' he asked gently.

The teacher smiled. 'I fell in love with Jesus,' he said. 'For many months I have known that the Bible is true, that Jesus is the son of God and that only those who believe in him and have their sins forgiven have any hope of going to heaven. But I was afraid what might happen to me if I became a public Christian. So I believed in my head, but wouldn't let my heart become involved. I knew if that happened I could no longer believe in secret. But day by day Jesus seemed to say to me, 'I love you. I love you so much I died for you.' And one day it hit my heart and I fell in love with Jesus. Now I want to be baptised.'

Ann had come into the room as the teacher began his story. The first he was aware of her presence was when she started to sob quietly. Tears of sheer joy ran down her face, and she looked radiant.

'Thank God,' she whispered. 'Our prayers are answered.'

On 18th July 1820 the teacher and another new believer, a woman, were baptised. The following day Adoniram and Ann left for Bengal. Over a hundred people stood on the river bank to wave them goodbye. And cries of 'Come back again' filled the air.

Just before darkness fell Adoniram wrote a note in his diary. *My heart is singing as I write this, and there is a sadness too. It has been thrilling to see believers born into the family of God, but it saddens me to leave them when they are so young in the faith. I feel as though I'm deserting them.*

The following day when he looked at what he'd written, Judson added another line or two. *What conceit! Imagine me feeling that I'm deserting our dear Burmese friends when God is with them! What could I do for them that God can't do a thousand times better. And, no matter how far I'm separated from them, I can pray for them every day. And I will.*

Ava, at last

It was six months before the Judsons returned to Rangoon. And there was good news and bad news awaiting them.

'We are ten believers now!' the Christians told them. 'But the teacher is having a hard time. Because he's such an influential man he's being persecuted by the authorities.'

'In what way?' Adoniram asked.

'There is a conspiracy against him. They say that he is trying to turn the bottom of the priest's rice pot upwards.'

Judson was struck by the analogy. It was quite true. If people believed in Jesus they would no longer give money to the priests.

The storyteller continued. 'But old Mya-day-men had an answer for them. He said 'So what? Let the priest turn it back again.'

Judson was pleased that Mya-day-men, who had returned to Rangoon some time before, was still sympathetic to Christians even if not to the Christian faith.

The time that followed their return was busy for the Judsons as well as for the new young church. The woman who had been baptised the day before they left started a small school for both boys and girls. People who were interested in the faith sent their children there so that they wouldn't be taught by the Buddhist priests. Converts started to use tracts, giving them to people who seemed interested in finding out more about the Lord Jesus. Adoniram completed his translation of Paul's letter to the Ephesians and did about half of the book of Acts. When each section of translation was completed it was sent to Hough in India for printing.

'There is too much for you to do on your own,' the teacher told Judson. 'And some of us are now able to take a bit of the load off your shoulders.'

Adoniram knew this was true. He was working too hard. Ann was also. And, when he thought about it, he realised that what his friend had said about the young Christians was true. Although they were all quite new converts some of them had grown in the faith at a remarkable speed. The church members discussed the issue and one of their number was appointed as assistant pastor. And that was done only just on time as both Adoniram and Ann became ill. Adoniram recovered slowly, but it was eventually decided that Ann would have to go abroad for treatment. It was with a sad heart that her husband saw her off, knowing that it could be a long time before they met again … if ever on this earth.

To take his mind off his problems Judson settled down to work, taking even less time off than he had done when Ann was in Rangoon. He was working on translation one day when there was a knock on the door of his room.

'The teacher needs to speak to you urgently. He is on his way to see you now.'

Adoniram, sensing that something was very wrong, prayed as he waited for the old man to come. And he didn't have long to wait.

'Please sit down,' he told his good friend when he came into the room.

'There is no time. I have come to say goodbye.'

Adoniram's heart sank.

'I've been warned that I will be killed if I remain in Rangoon, and my family too. So I have hired a river-boat and they're already on it. We're moving away down the Irrawaddy. But what an opportunity to spread the good news about Jesus! Please may I have a supply of tracts to take with me so that I can be a missionary there? Perhaps you will visit us one day and find a new church.'

All sadness left Judson. Sure, he would miss his good friend, but this was how it ought to be. Converts should become missionaries themselves, and they should move out and on.

The two men knelt and prayed, held each other close, and said goodbye.

As he left the mission house the teacher looked back only once. 'If I don't see you again on earth,' he told Adoniram, 'I will see you in heaven.'

Some months after the teacher left, a new missionary couple arrived. Dr Jonathan Price, his wife and baby daughter, came fresh from America. He soon had a thriving medical practice up and running, and he became especially well known for his cataract surgery. Sadly his wife and child died of fever before they had been long in Burma. When that happened he threw himself into his work more than ever.

'The Golden Ears have heard about your operations,' a messenger told the young doctor one day.

'And the Golden Lips wish you to appear at the Golden Feet.'

Price was thrown by this invitation, which there was no question of refusing. Rather than let the doctor travel alone, Adoniram went with him. The two men had plenty of time to talk as the oarsmen plied their way up the Irrawaddy to Ava.

'Tell me the story of your work in Burma,' Price asked.

Adoniram started at the beginning, with the group meeting for prayer under the haystack years before, then brought him right up to date. 'So,' concluded his history lesson, 'we worked for six years before our first convert came to faith. Now, after ten years in Burma, there are eighteen believers.'

The young doctor looked thoughtful. 'It's not many to show for all that work.'

Judson thought hard before replying. 'The Bible tells us that the angels in heaven rejoice when one sinner comes to Jesus. The rejoicing of angels eighteen times in ten years is no small thing. In any case,' he added, 'other work has been done too. Children are being taught in a Christian school away from the teaching of the Buddhist monks. All four gospels have been translated into Burmese as well as the Acts of the Apostles, Romans and others of Paul's letters too. Many hundreds of tracts and booklets have been distributed.'

'I'm sorry,' Price said. 'So much has been achieved. There are ministers back home in America who've worked for many more years than ten and who've not done nearly so much.'

Price was overwhelmed when he saw the grandeur of the Golden Palace at Ava, although Adoniram had tried to describe it to him. And even though he had been warned, the young doctor was still taken by surprise when everyone fell to the floor as if dead when King Bagyidaw entered the Golden Hall.

'Is this the eye doctor?' the king demanded.

His officials confirmed that this was who Price was.

'Tell me what you do to give blind people back their sight.'

Still kneeling on the floor some distance from the Golden Throne, Price did his best to describe a cataract operation.

King Bagyidaw listened carefully. Blindness caused by cataract was a real problem in Burma. Suddenly he lost interest in what was being said.

'I will see you again,' he announced. 'Go.'

The two men reversed, still on their knees, out of the Golden Presence.

On their second visit to the Golden Feet, the Golden Lips asked still more questions about eye surgery. Then it seemed the king noticed Adoniram for the very first time.

'What is that?' he asked, as though he had just seen a speck of dirt on the golden floor.

An official explained who Judson was and what he did.

'Have any Burmese believed in your god?'

The missionary admitted that they had, not knowing what to expect by way of reaction.

'How do you tell them about your god?'

Judson explained that he preached.

'Preach now!' ordered the Golden Lips.

Kneeling in that great golden hall, a little distance from the Golden Feet, and with his hands held together as a mark of respect, Adoniram Judson preached to the king of Burma.

Suddenly, and without saying a word, the Golden Presence departed, and Judson was cut short mid-sentence.

A few days later a messenger came from the Golden Lips, telling Price that he could not leave Ava, and giving Adoniram a piece of land for a Kyoung, a holy place. On 25th January 1823, Judson left for Rangoon, there to work until Ann returned. He was convinced that they should then move to Ava, a city with a population of about 700,000, rather than remain in the small town of Rangoon. With the favour of the king, Judson thought there was more opportunity to preach the gospel there. In any case, the new Christians in Rangoon were now ready to run their own church.

But when he arrived back home it was to discover that there were only four converts at the mission house, that one had died, and that others had moved away. God gave time for the little church to build up again, for Ann did not get back from her long trip to America for medical treatment until nearly Christmas. They had been separated for twenty-seven months, and Adoniram had not heard from his wife for the last ten of them. With Ann came two new and enthusiastic missionaries who had been studying Burmese with her as their teacher throughout their long voyage from America. Their arrival and their fair knowledge of the language allowed the Judsons to leave Rangoon for Ava with an easy mind. The work would go on.

'What a sight those boats must have been!' Adoniram laughed, as he and his wife relaxed together on the river-boat.

Ann smiled. 'You should have seen their faces! I'd told them about the golden everything to do with Burmese royalty, but they were not prepared to find their trip up the Irrawaddy to Rangoon interrupted by a fleet of golden boats!'

'It has its funny side, but it could have been serious.'

'I know that. The situation between England and Burma is such that if you look as though you could be English and you speak the language too, albeit the American version, things could be tricky. I think it helped to persuade them that we were Americans when I could do the persuading in fluent Burmese.'

Ann was excited at the prospect of having greater freedom in Ava, as it seemed would be the case in the future. But the encouragement her husband had had when he was at the Golden Feet was all they were ever to get. And there was sad news too. Mya-day-men had died. His widow came to see Ann and found comfort in their friendship.

Ava was a quieter city than when Judson had last been there. King Bagyidaw had moved the royal court to Amarapura, five miles upriver.

'I can't believe that our little house has been built in just two weeks,' Ann said. 'But I must confess I'll be glad not to continue living on the boat. It was beginning to feel rather cramped.'

'You'll certainly have more room now,' Adoniram smiled at his wife. 'Would three rooms and a veranda on one metre high stilts suit m'lady?'

'It certainly would!'

'And I'll start right away to build a brick house. We'll need that in the summer heat.'

Thinking how stuffy wooden houses can become, Ann agreed heartily.

While some things went to plan, other things did not.

'I don't know what to think about Price,' Ann said in a worried tone some months later.

'When we came to Ava he seemed to be doing so well. If I remember correctly there were nearly twenty at the service in his home on our first Sunday here.'

'That's right. We felt so encouraged.'

'But when that cataract operation failed and left the poor Siamese woman blind, I think he married her to compensate for what he had done to her.'

'That's how I feel. As if a doctor could never have a failed operation!'

'It seems you can't in Burma. I suspect Price thought he'd be disposed of if the news got out.'

'And would he?'

'Quite likely he would.'

'The sad thing is,' Ann concluded, 'it's as though he's suffering some sort of depression. He has just lost heart. It seems more important to him nowadays to get on with those in authority than it does to preach the gospel.'

'Adoniram,' his wife said one day after they were well settled in Ava. 'We really must give these two dear little girls a home. It's not their fault that their mother is mentally ill and can't look after them. And their father wouldn't have asked us for help if he'd been at all able to cope.'

Judson looked at her and thought of the girls who had stayed with them for the last few weeks. 'Perhaps they will fill the space in our hearts and home that we hoped would be filled with children of our own?'

That comment caused Ann several minutes of troubled thought before she replied.

'They may do that,' she admitted. 'But I honestly love the girls for themselves not as replacements for our lost baby and dear Roger.'

Mary and Abby (those were the new names they were given when they became part of the Judson family) took some time to recover from the trauma of living with their mother's mental illness. But in time they warmed to the love and care that surrounded them in the mission house. Ann ran a school for them and for one other child.

It was when they were settling in Ava that the Judsons met Henry Crouger, an Englishman who had come to Ava to make his fortune.

'I've done well since I came here,' he told his new friends. 'I'm in the meat trade.'

Adoniram looked surprised. 'There can't be any money in selling meat to Buddhists who don't eat the stuff.'

Crouger just laughed. 'You're wrong there! Buddhists won't kill animals, but they will eat animals that die naturally. Well, a lot of animals just happen to die naturally in the basement of my house. And for people who don't kill, the Burmese are very fond of their meat when they can get it!'

It would have been hard to find two more different men, but Judson and Crouger became friends.

After the service on Sunday, 23rd May 1824, news

came that Britain and Burma were at war and that the British had taken Rangoon. It was with sad hearts that the Judsons agreed to have no more contact with Crouger for the time being because he was English. And it seemed the decision was taken only just in time as Crouger was arrested and imprisoned. But both Price and Judson were immediately suspect because the authorities discovered they had received money from the Englishman, and they concluded it was payment for spying. In fact they had only used him as a convenient way of cashing cheques they had been sent. Things looked bleak.

Death Prison

'Prison Diary - Adoniram Judson - 18th June 1824

As it may be that I won't get out of prison alive I'm going to keep a diary while I'm here. Perhaps it will get out even if I don't. How much I'll be able to write I don't know, but I'll do what I can.

Two days ago we were in the mission house preparing to eat our evening meal. Suddenly there was a dreadful commotion and the house door flew open. In rushed a government official complete with his black book, and behind him were the Spotted Faces. Mary and Abby got such a fright that they started screaming. Ann, who can cope with most things, had a job preventing herself joining in with them. The Spotted Faces are the most feared of all the government's men. They are recruited from the prisons and their job is to put other people behind bars. Only the most dangerous inmates have spots tattooed on their faces. Most of them are murderers or have committed other violent crimes, and they have no conscience about murdering others in the so-called cause of justice. Hence Ann's and the girls' reaction to their appearance.

'You are called by the king,' the official informed me, that being the correct formula of arrest.

Immediately I was thrown to the ground. It seemed that the king who had called me had sent his thugs to make sure

I answered his call, which may be why they tied my elbows behind my back until I thought my shoulders were dislocated. They hadn't dragged me very far down the road when Maung Ing rushed up behind us, Ann having put together some money by way of a bribe so that they would loosen the rope. They took the money, threw me to the ground yet again, and tightened the rope to breaking point. Even the chief jailer was angry at the force they had used, despite the fact he has 'murderer' written on his forehead - a common punishment for crimes here being to brand the offender with his crime.

Because the prison was only lit by tiny oil lamps it took me a while to see who else is here. Poor Crouger is in the stocks, and so is Rogers, who thought he was well in with the king. Price was brought in shortly after me. He looked dazed and confused by what was happening to him. The chief jailer insists on us addressing him as 'Father', and that sticks in my throat as he wouldn't treat vermin as viciously as he's treating us.

The nights are appalling. It's going to be hard putting it down in writing, but I'm going to do it so that if this diary is found by someone with a scrap of human kindness prison conditions might improve. Before nightfall those who have their feet in stocks (and that's nearly everyone, men and a few women too) have the chains that are on their ankles all the time hooked into a pulley contraption which is then hoisted in the air until we are left almost dangling from it, our feet strung high up and only our shoulders on the ground. We thought we'd be left like that for a short time then released, but we were hung all of that night and last night too. 'Father' comes in, wishes us goodnight in a sickeningly sweet way, then orders the pulleys up.

I can't describe the pain of the pulleys. At first our heads heat up, and our necks, and we feel as though they will burst. Then it's a choice of pain - we can concentrate on the aching numbness of our feet and legs, or the screaming pain from thigh, back and shoulder muscles, or the explosion that's going on inside our heads. But in the morning when we're let loose and the blood drains back into our lower limbs it is as though they are filled with boiling oil. And that's all I can write. I may have to go through it for as long as I'm here, and I can't bear to think about it during the day as well as enduring it every night.

Yesterday and today Maung Ing came with food for me, and brought some for other prisoners too. No food is provided and the authorities would be quite happy if we died of starvation. We are reckoned to be spies, so the death sentence seems inevitable.

Dearest Ann, if ever you get this diary I want you to know what a comfort it is to think about you, even when I'm strung up at night. I picture your hazel eyes and I try to see your smile too. But that's hard. I know that your love for me means that you'll be weeping not smiling, knowing what I'm going through. God bless you, my sweet one. I know you're praying for me as I am for you.

25th June 1824

I was able to speak to the faithful Maung Ing when he brought my food today. Apparently the magistrate and one of his thugs went back to the mission house the day after I was arrested and announced he would return the following day to search the place. Ann hunted the house for anything written in English, and therefore potentially implicated in spying, and burned the lot. The translation work she bundled up, wrapped it in thick material, and buried it in the garden as far from the house as she could! She didn't stop there. My resourceful wife went to the highest official she could think of, taking $100 with her, and extracted from him an agreement written on a banana leaf that she could visit me in prison. It was wonderful to see her, but how I hated Ann seeing me in this terrible place, especially as she is now carrying our much longed for baby.

Will I ever see that cherished child? Will I be home in heaven before our baby is born on earth? Poor Ann, having to go through all this alone. Thank God for Maung Ing, Mary and Abby. (There is even a little humour in the account of the raid on the mission house - Ann made the raiders tea and insisted they drank it!)

August 1824

I've been in Death Prison for about two months now. We've tried to keep track of the date, but there is some disagreement about it. I must remember to ask Maung Ing when he brings my food tomorrow. Ann was given permission to visit today. Nobody will ever know what it felt like to be so weak that I had to crawl along the ground to meet her. Not only that, I am utterly filthy and have no way of bathing. I could see my dear wife bracing herself and she coped as she always does. But what can it have been like for her to see me soiled, in rags, chained and too weak to stand? God has sent Maung Ing for such a time as this, otherwise she and the girls would have been at the mercy of unspeakable men. That's a blessing, and I'm trying to count my blessings. But it's hard.

Next day

Once or twice, when I have been near to total despair, God has done something to assure me that he is still there, that he does still love me, and that he is still in total control. For a time the European prisoners have been allowed to have pillows. Today Maung Ing brought a pillow from Ann. It's a rough brown scratchy affair, bumpy and very uncomfortable. There is no way the guards could have guessed the comfort it would bring me. Inside is all my translation work, all that exists in the world of the Bible in Burmese! This has given me hope in this hopeless place.

Beginning October, 1824

My dear resourceful wife! For the last few weeks she has been writing me short letters which she has folded into tiny squares and slipped into my food - hidden in a vegetable cake and well covered with rice! Today I had a longer letter. It was rolled up and stuck down the spout of the teapot Maung Ing brought full of tea! The tea was good though it was lukewarm, but the letter made me feel human again.

Two weeks later

'Father,' as he insists on being called, has concocted yet another means of striking fear into our hearts. Each day at exactly 3 pm a gong is banged. Two Spotted Faces march in, walk among the prisoners, then stand in front of two of them. These poor souls are then made to shuffle out of the prison, their legs held in three sets of chains, to their death. As 3 pm draws near each day there is a terror such as I could never have imagined.

Some days I just wish they would stand in front of me. Then it would be all over. Thoughts of heaven sometimes make me long for death. Thoughts of Ann and our unborn child chain me to the world.

20th December 1824

Today Ann was allowed to see me, though how she now recognises me I do not know. I have never been heavy, but now I can count the bones in my hands and feet through the loose skin. Even if I survive this I don't know if my muscles will ever function properly again. They may have permanently wasted away.

21st December

This has been the worst day of my life. My darling wife, now nearly at the time for our child's birth, must be despairing in the mission house. Today she was allowed to visit for longer than usual. From somewhere she'd got buffalo meat and had made a pie with it for me. Why did that break my heart? Why couldn't I swallow even one mouthful of it? Why did everything in me reject her work ... her love? Have I become incapable of responding? Am I still human or has this hideous place done its work? Am I dead without ever dying? God help me!

1st January 1825

I have just realised that it is the first day of the new year. It seems that I am to live to be a father once again as the child must come soon. My precious wife is working for me still. Maung Ing tells me that she visits the city governor's wife to secure small favours for us. It's through her that we foreign prisoners are allowed out of the shed into small bamboo shelters for a short time each day. But the heartlessness of it! We are taken out on time to hear the 3 pm gong and to see two of our brother prisoners dragged to their death. It is a piece of theatre at which we are a captive audience.

Sometimes I think I can't pray at all now, but today I realised that when I cry out to God to help me it's the most fervent prayer I've prayed in all my life!

26th January 1825

Never have I felt so grateful and so utterly useless. Maung Ing came today to tell me that I have a daughter. And what has she for a father? I am of no use to her or to Ann or to anyone else. And even as I write this I see I'm so self-pitying that I'm making myself of no use to God either. I'm going to thank God over and over again until I can stir up some feeling of thankfulness in my heart. Thank you for Ann's safe delivery. Thank you for a live child. Thank you, Jesus. Thank you for all you've done for me. Thank you for the Cross and for all you suffered there for me. Thank you that you know and remember what it is to suffer terribly. Thank you, thank you, thank you, thank you. Please help me to feel thankful. I've so much to be thankful for even in this terrible place.

15th February 1825

I have seen my daughter. This afternoon Ann arrived at the prison gate carrying Maria, our tiny scrap of a child. She seems to have as little flesh on her as I have, and Ann has no more. Just for a minute I could imagine that we were together, our

*family of three. Ann pressed me to hold Maria despite the foul
state I'm in. I could see from Ann's eyes that she needed me to
do that, so pushing away thoughts of what the dirt that clings
to me could do to such a frail infant, I held her and I loved her.
We prayed over our daughter and committed her to the one who
holds all things in his hands. And when they left I missed her. I
missed my own Maria.*

16th February

    *Last night, strung up in the pulley as usual, I thought of my
child. And in the midst of the ugliness and brutality of this place
something beautiful happened. I was able to compose a lullaby
for my sweet Maria, though an odd lullaby. And when Ann is
next able to come I'll give it to her to sing to our daughter.*

    Sleep, darling infant, sleep;
    Hushed on thy mother's breast;
    Let no rude sound of clanking chains
    Disturb thy balmy rest.
    How can tenderness and beauty come from such
    a place as this? Only by God's grace.

In March that year all the foreign prisoners were called
out into the yard. The chief jailer, who still insisted on
being called 'Father,' had two more shackles added to
the three they already wore. Spotted Faces demolished
the bamboo shelters the Europeans had built and their
pillows were taken away, Adoniram's included. The last
he saw of the rough brown bundle it was being thrown
into the prison rubbish heap. Had he had time to think

about its loss he would have cried out with the pain of it, but he did not. So much was happening.

When Ann heard of these further trials she went to the city governor's wife and begged her to say a word on behalf of the prisoners. On her next visit she built another bamboo shack for her husband, doing it all herself as he was too ill, exhausted and weak to help her. It was tiny, too low for him to stand in. But it didn't need to be any higher as he was nearly unable to stand anyway. No sooner had she finished her building work than the Spotted Faces came and chased her away.

'Father' looked on and then barked an order. 'Tie them in twos!' As soon as he saw that Ann was out of earshot. 'March them to the courthouse.'

There was the clanking of further chains and anguished groans. Men, more dead than alive, were dragged to their feet and pushed at knife-point towards the courthouse. Any who fell, and several did, were kicked until they somehow made it to their feet, then half-dragged, half-pushed. There were eight of them altogether, and they looked more like skinned rabbits than human beings.

'The foreigners have all been taken away,' was the first Ann heard of what had happened.

Frantic with fear she ran round the streets near the prison.

'Have you seen foreign prisoners?' she begged of everyone she met.

Most shook their heads, too afraid of the Spotted

Faces to admit seeing anything.

Ann ran from one to the other - asking, begging, shaking with the fear of what might have happened. Running across the narrow space between two pagodas she nearly knocked down an old woman.

'Have you seen foreign prisoners being moved?' she wept.

Shuffling up the narrow lane, the woman signalled to Ann to come with her. Realising the danger she might be causing, she followed the retreating figure into the shadow of the pagoda until they could not be seen from the road.

'Tell me what you've seen?', Ann begged.

From underneath a scarf a lined old face looked into hers. 'Yes, I saw them,' the woman said. 'They were dragging them towards the Mootangai.'

Thanking her, Ann raced back down to the road. 'The Mootangai!' she thought as she ran. 'If they get a boat on the Mootangai they'll be on the Irrawaddy and away and I'll not know where to look for them!'

Shaking with fear and exhaustion, she raced back to the governor's house. His wife saw Ann coming and ran to meet her.

'They're still alive,' she said. 'And they're being taken to Amarapura.'

Oung-pen-la

The day after the prisoners were moved the mission house was in a flurry of activity. Koo-chil, the Judsons' Bengali cook, wrapped rice in banana leaves and packed them into a basket. Mary collected together the things Ann thought they would need. And Abby sat on the floor rocking Maria from side to side, trying to settle her to sleep.

'We'll need to leave for Amarapura right away,' Ann said urgently, to encourage them to hurry. 'It's blazing hot, and they might not give the prisoners enough to drink. They could die in this heat if they make them march.'

The thought of Adoniram dying spurred them on. There was no question of waiting until the raging sun went down, so the little huddle of people, laden with all they could carry, sweated their way to the Mootangai where they hired a boat to take them to Amarapura.

Maung Ing, who was left to look after the mission house, prayed for them as they went.

They met Crouger's servant when they reached the river.

'They're still alive,' he called, running along the track to the waterside. 'One prisoner died as they marched, but Mr Judson and the others are in the prison at Amarapura.'

Ann was worried. 'How are they? How did they cope with walking when they are all so weak?'

'I ran and caught up with them,' the servant told her. 'And when I saw the state of their feet I unwrapped my turban, tore it into four pieces, and wrapped Mr Judson and Mr Crouger's feet up to stop them being badly cut as they walked.'

'God bless you,' Ann said, truly thankful for what the man had done.

'This is as far as I can take you,' the boatman told them, when they got near to Amarapura.

The weary little group climbed from the boat and set out to walk the short distance to the town. Asking Koo-chil to care for the children, Ann ran ahead. But the others had not even reached the first of the houses when she came running back along the road, tears coursing down her face.

'They're not there!' she said, trying to stifle her tears. 'They've been moved to Oung-pen-la, and that's too far for us to walk.'

Seeing how weary Ann was, and how baby Maria was needing to be fed, Koo-chil took charge. He left them sheltering under a tree and went to find a cart to take them to the prison where Adoniram and the others were being held. The cart he brought back with him looked as weary as the group who climbed into it. But it got there, creaking and rattling as it went.

'They cannot be here!', Koo-chil said, as they approached the prison at Oung-pen-la. 'This place is derelict.'

The sound of coughing broke through the air. It came from inside the tumbledown walls.

'They ARE here!' Mary and Abby shouted together. 'Papa Judson IS here!'

Leaving the children sitting in the cart, Koo-chil and Ann went to investigate. Seven prisoners were chained inside the ruins of the prison. The broken down walls could not keep them in, but their chains could. Yet even they were not needed, for none of the men had the strength to move. Adoniram's sunken eyes lit up when he saw his wife and cook climb through the rubble. While Ann sat on the ground holding her husband's emaciated hand in hers, Koo-chil fed him small mouthfuls of rice from a banana leaf, then fed those who were with him too.

'Oh no! Please no!' the voice rang through the cool air a few hours later.

Ann, who heard it from the jailer's grain shed which she had persuaded him to lend her for shelter, left Koo-chil and the children and ran to see what was happening. To her horror she discovered that the same pulley arrangement had been erected at Oung-pen-la, and the seven prisoners were strung up with their feet in the air and only the backs of their heads and shoulders resting on the ground. It was some time before she was able to go back to the grain shed. She needed to cry and she needed to pray, and she needed to be apart for a while. But Maria didn't understand. And when she was hungry and yelled for her milk, Ann had to pull herself together and go back to the children.

They had not been long at Oung-pen-la when Mary came out in a rash.

'I'm not feeling well, Mamma,' she told Ann one morning. 'I'm hot and sticky, and I've got spots.'

Ann undressed the little girl and looked at the angry rash on her skin.

'This will help cool it down,' she said, sponging her with cool water.

But Ann's heart was racing. She recognised the signs of smallpox, and she knew that could be a killer.

'I've got to act quickly,' Ann thought, 'for the sake of the other children.'

'Mary dear,' she said, cradling the sick child's head on her knee. 'I need to explain something to you. You have a disease called smallpox which Abby and Maria will catch too unless you can help me stop it.'

The girl asked what she could do.

'Will you let me prick one of your nasty spots?'

Mary nodded weakly.

'Then I'll prick Abby and Maria with the same needle. That should prevent them from taking smallpox badly.'

Looking at her sister and the baby but feeling very fearful, Mary said that Ann could prick her. The jailer's wife watched Ann inoculating the children and asked her to do her family too. Then the village children were brought along to be treated. Poor little Mary endured the pricks because she knew she was helping the others. Abby and the village children caught a mild dose of smallpox but Maria took the illness badly and was very, very poorly. Ann was so grateful that Crouger's servant came every few days with food, for she had her hands full looking after Mary and Maria.

'There's a big cart coming with a lion in it!' Abby shouted. 'It is being taken to the prison!'

Koo-chil went to investigate. He wore a very worried expression when he returned to the grain store. 'She's right,' he said in an awed voice, 'except that it's not a lion, it's a lioness. And she's growling with hunger.'

Ann fell to her knees. 'Please, Lord, please don't let them be fed to the lioness. Father, you prevented the lions eating Daniel and his friends in the Bible, please please don't let this creature eat the prisoners.'

Abby's eyes and mouth were wide open in fear. Fortunately Mary and Maria were asleep. Ann took the frightened girl on to her knee. 'Papa Judson has told you the story of Daniel in the lions' den, hasn't he?'

The child nodded.

'Did the lions eat Daniel and his friends?'

Abby shook her head.

'Well,' Ann told her with a conviction that surprised her, 'you and I will pray that God will shut the mouth of this lioness too.'

And several days later the lioness's mouth was shut for ever. The jailer, not having been given orders to feed her, left her to starve to death.

All that Ann had done was too much for her frail body and she became so ill that Adoniram was allowed out of prison to help care for her and to find a village woman who could feed their starving little daughter.

'There's a bad rumour,' Koo-chil told Judson, in the midst of the problems.

'What's that?'

'They say the war is not going well and that prisoners are to be buried alive to please the gods and make them give Burma victory.'

'God help us!' the American prayed.

And he did.

As the summer passed Ann regained her strength and Maria clung to life, though at times only just. It was in August that a cart arrived at Oung-pen-la to collect the prisoners.

'Where are they being taken?' Koo-chil asked the jailer.

'The king needs them in Amarapura,' he was told. 'He has a job for the foreigners to do.'

Koo-chil ran to tell Ann the news.

'If they've a job to do,' she told her cook, 'that means they're not to be killed.'

When the weary little family found their way to Amarapura they discovered that the king did indeed need the prisoners. The war was coming to an end and a peace treaty was being prepared. The king of Burma needed men who could read both Burmese and English to work out the terms of the treaty.

The peace treaty kept Adoniram and his fellow prisoners busy for some months. They were treated well when they were needed, and sent back to prison and ill-treated when they were not. Ann struggled to cope with her little family and the work of the mission. Maung Ing, that faithful Christian, was a huge support to her. 'God's gift,' she called him over and over again. But even that terrible summer had a time of joy in it. When Adoniram returned for a brief visit to the mission house he discovered that his pillow, his precious translation stuffed pillow, had been recovered. The work of many years had not been lost! Weak and weary though they were, they felt great happiness that day.

On the very last day of the year 1825, Adoniram Judson was finally released from prison into the safety and comfort of British protection. When Ann was fit to travel their journey down the Irrawaddy was very different from when they went up. This time they travelled on golden boats to Rangoon.

'It's just a ruin now,' Ann said sadly, when they arrived at the mission house.

Her husband looked at it and shook his head. 'This isn't the place for us any more,' he said. I think Amherst would be the best place to work. And we've been invited to go there. I've even been asked to read a Bible passage at the dedication of the new city.'

'Amherst?'

'Yes. The peace treaty agreed that the British should build the new city and the work's well underway. We'd be able to work there in safety.'

When Ann thought about it, she agreed that it seemed a good idea.

Plans were made for the move, and the Judsons went to Amherst along with four Burmese Christian families, including the faithful Maung Ing. But Adoniram's work on the treaty was not quite finished and he left his family in the care of the Christians there and went back to Ava for a time. Four months after leaving Ann at Amherst, Adoniram wrote an emotional entry in his diary.

Today I received a letter dated 18th October. A man brought it upriver to me. When I saw its black seal my heart sank as I thought my sweet Maria had lost her battle for life. But nothing could have prepared me for the contents, a copy of which follow.

"My dear Sir, To one who has suffered so much and with exemplary fortitude, there needs but little preface to tell a tale of distress. It is cruel to torture you with doubt and suspense. To sum up the unhappy tidings in a few words - Mrs Judson is no more."

I have lost the one who, under God, has been everything to me. My only comfort is that my darling Ann is at home in heaven with Jesus. But on this earth there seems no comfort at all. I cannot begin to imagine never seeing her dear face again, or that for those last four weeks when I've been thinking about her, she has been cold in the grave. My heart is broken.

The winter that followed brought sadness upon sadness. Adoniram arrived back in Amherst at the beginning of 1827. A few days after his return Abby died, and on 24th April Maria died too. She was two years and three months old. Judson's way of coping with his great burden of sadness was to throw himself into his work in a frenzy. And that is what he did.

Adoniram established a new work in the town of Moulmein, and before many months had passed there was a zayat where people could come to find out about Jesus. A Burmese Christian was in charge of a second zayat, one which taught reading. Maung Ing and another man looked after a preaching zayat and two schools were also established, one for boys and one for girls. Each zayat was in a different shed and all were within a mission compound. But the rush of activity only covered Judson's grief for a time and he went through a very bad patch several months long.

'I'm useless,' Judson told a colleague. 'I've no heart for anything.'

'Shhh,' the man whispered, 'listen.' Adoniram would have moved away into the solitude he felt he needed, but his friend held him back.

A Burmese Christian had a group of young men around him. 'I am fifty years old,' he told them, 'and I was brought up in a wild jungle tribe. We were not farmers or traders. Our living was robbery and murder. It breaks my heart to confess it, but I was involved in over thirty murders myself. No wonder the authorities were anxious to break up the tribe, and when they did I was sold as a slave. If my new owner had known about my temper he'd never have bought me. It was after that I met Mr Judson and heard about the Lord Jesus. Can you imagine my astonishment when I discovered that the Lord could forgive all my sins? Even mine! I still can't quite take it in. But I know it's true, because I've read it in the Bible for myself.'

He handed the young men leaflets about the Christian faith.

'God has used you,' Judson's colleague told his depressed friend. 'And God will use you again.'

Adoniram shook his head and walked off into the shadows, his shoulders stooped and his head held low.

'I think we should leave him alone.' It was George Boardman who spoke. He and his wife Sarah had arrived in Moulmein in early 1828, fifteen months after Ann Judson died. 'He's a child of God and our Heavenly Father will see him through this dark tunnel.'

'But what does he do in the jungle all day?' his wife asked.

'I've followed him out, and he does the same every day. He walks to an old ruined pagoda and sits there until it's almost nightfall then he walks slowly home again.'

'Is it safe for him?' Sarah felt anxious for their friend.

'Yes,' her husband assured her. 'An elder follows him into the jungle each morning and keeps watch over him. He's going to build a seat in the ruins and put a canopy over it to give Adoniram shade.'

And although that was done, Judson never mentioned it. For forty days he sat alone in the jungle, then little by little he began to recover and to work again.

The Boardman family grew with the birth of their son. In their big-heartedness they also adopted Dr Price's two boys when their father died. But George Boardman himself was ill, coughing ominously with what sounded like tuberculosis. He worked for as long as his health allowed, then died of the disease. Sarah, a woman with a true missionary heart, did not return to America but remained in Burma doing whatever she was able to do.

'I've shut myself up here for two whole years,' Judson told a friend at the end of 1832, 'but that's it finished. The very last page of the New Testament is now translated into Burmese! Praise the Lord!'

Some time later Adoniram went to see the printing process which had been transferred back to Burma.

'How large is the printing house?' he asked, looking around him.

'It's fifty feet long. It needs to be to house both presses.'

Adoniram walked around the place studying the bundles of printed papers. 'How much have you printed since you came here?'

His friend laughed. 'I can tell you that exactly. In the last year we've printed 3000 New Testaments, 33,000 tracts and books of questions and answers, including some in Karen and Taling, and a Karen spelling book too.'

'And to think how it all began,' Judson said. 'How good God is!'

Work took up all of Adoniram's time. If he didn't work he felt badly the loneliness of where Ann used to be, so he worked hard.

When Sarah's letter arrived early in 1834, he put his papers aside to read it.

'I must tell you how much your translation of the New Testament is helping me,' she wrote. 'Until now I've been reading in English and so still thinking in English. But the longing of my heart is to draw as close as I can to our Burmese brothers and sisters, and your translation is helping me to do so ...'

For the two months that followed the arrival of Sarah's letter, Adoniram prayed. And the subject of his prayer was marriage. Could it be that God intended him to marry again? Would Sarah have him? He was forty six and she was still a young woman. What was he to do?

His prayers were answered and his loneliness dispelled on 10th April 1834 when he and Sarah Boardman married, committing themselves to God, to each other and to the Burmese people.

A second happiness

Sarah took her new young Burmese helper into the mission house. The girl looked round about her, and with a typical lack of embarrassment she went from room to room doing a tour of inspection.

'It's just like one of our houses!' she said, surprised at the discovery. 'We also have three rooms and a separate cookhouse on stilts. Your thatched roof is just like ours, and your walls are also made of bamboo matting. All that's different is that you have two little extra rooms where Mr Judson works and Maung Ing sleeps.'

'What did you expect?' Sarah laughed.

The girl thought for a minute. 'I imagined your house would be better than ours and full of expensive things.'

Sitting her young friend down, the pair of them talked as Sarah made them tea. 'Missionaries don't need special houses because they're not special people.' Seeing the surprise on her visitor's face, she went on. 'They are just messengers. God has given us the Bible which is his message to everyone in the world, and our job is to be messengers, to take his Bible to every country of the world, to translate it into every language in the world, and to tell every person in the world about Jesus.'

'Is that why you learned to speak Burmese?'

'That's right. And that's why I'm now learning Karen.'

'Will you tell me about your Jesus?' the girl asked shyly.

A smile crossed Sarah's face. 'I certainly will,' she said. 'He's my best friend and I love telling people about him.'

'You Christians!' the young girl exclaimed. 'You must like being together when you build all your houses so close. It must be because you all love this Jesus?'

Only when Koo-chil came in from the cookhouse to tell the family that the rice was cooked, did the girl leave the mission house and weave her way through the zayats and shacks in the compound. Sarah gazed after her wondering what the young girl was now thinking about. It was amazing to see how the Burmese Christians were reaching out to their Buddhist neighbours - even their lives told their friends and families about Jesus.

Young George Boardman, who had been just two when his father died, was now six years old. It was time to decide about his health and education.

'We've both lost loved ones to the diseases of Burma,' Adoniram said to his wife, as they discussed the matter.

Sad memories came tumbling back into Sarah's mind. 'I know that. And I'm thinking the same as you are. Would it be best to send George back to America to be looked after by the family there? It's a much healthier climate and it would allow him to have regular schooling.'

The prospect of how empty their home would be without him caused Judson some thought. But to risk losing George to disease? There was no real choice, and plans were made for his passage. Difficult though it was to think of sending the child they loved to the other side of the world, they believed that was best for him.

'Let's fill a memory box for you to take with you,' Sarah suggested to the little boy. 'We'll put things in it to remind you of your home here, of your mamma and papa, of Maung Ing and Koo-chil.'

'I want to remember my friends too,' George said. 'What can I take to remind me of them?'

'Let's go and see.'

The two of them walked round the mission compound and showed the memory box to the children they met.

'Can I have something to remember you by?' George asked each one of them.

'This smooth stone will remind you of me,' one said. 'It's the stone we found at the river side.'

A girl came running up with a small quill pen. 'Will this fit in the box? It's the one I learned to write with.'

'You can have my model monkey,' his best friend said. 'I made it out of clay.'

By bedtime that night George had collected a box of memories to take all the way to America. And the memory he left with his mother and stepfather was of a little boy sound asleep in his bamboo bed clutching a wooden box.

All the work Adoniram and Sarah could push into each day didn't fill the space George left. But the work they got through was amazing. Sarah studied Taling so that she could translate tracts and Ann's question and answer book into that language. Adoniram revised and corrected his Old and New Testament translations. He preached seven times most weeks, and Sarah organised prayer meetings and women's meetings. There was never a dull moment.

'Mr Judson,' Koo-chil said. 'May I speak to you?'

Adoniram, a little puzzled by the interruption, closed his book. It was usually Sarah with whom Koo-chil discussed the mission house food. 'Of course,' he said. 'Come in and sit down.'

The Bengali sat but didn't seem to be able to find the words he wanted to say.

'What did you want to talk about?' the missionary asked gently, noticing tears glinting in his cook's eyes. 'Is something wrong?'

Koo-chil shook his head, wiped his eyes, and began his story.

'I was brought up a Buddhist, and I have gone through life frightened of so many things. As a child I was afraid of evil spirits, and would have died of that fear if I'd not had my spirit strings on to protect me.'

Judson wondered what was coming next.

'And when I came to work for you I thought you were so reckless, you didn't seem to worry about offending the spirits. You gave no money to priests when they came begging, and you didn't leave out offerings for the spirits either. When I discovered that I nearly ran away. But then I watched you. When things went wrong you didn't blame evil spirits, you prayed to your God. And even when you were taken away to Death Prison Mrs Judson didn't go to the priest with money to ward off spirits.'

Remembering Ann's faithfulness, Adoniram could understand why she'd made such an impression on the cook.

Koo-chil's eyes were shining again, but not with tears. He went on with his story.

'It was when you were in Oung-pen-la that I really began to think. I decided that if Mrs Judson could go though all that happened then, and you too, and still not be frightened of evil spirits, then your God must be more powerful than all the spirits. I talked about it to Mrs Judson and she told me about Jesus. But do you know what spoke to my heart? When she was telling me about Jesus, baby Maria was terribly ill and looked as though she would not survive. Yet Mrs Judson still believed God loved her. But when your wife died my heart broke and I decided that your god was not good after all. But I was wrong. And when I realised I was wrong I said sorry to God and asked him to forgive me.'

Adoniram's face shone as the story unfolded.

'And he did forgive me,' Koo-chil said. 'He has taken away all my fear of evil spirits and filled me with feelings of thankfulness. Now I want everyone to know about it and have come to ask for baptism.'

The cook was surprised at his employer's reaction. He'd not often been given a bear hug, nor had he often seen a man cry with sheer joy.

On 31st October 1835 Adoniram opened his Bible at the very front page. On it there was a list of names and dates. He read them over.

8th February 1812 -
Ann Hasseltine married Adoniram Judson
22nd June 1813 -
Our first child born dead and buried at sea
11th September 1815 -
Roger born - died April 1816
26th January 1825 -
Maria born - died 24th April 1827
18th October 1826 -
Ann Hasseltine Judson died
10th April 1834 -
Sarah Boardman married Adoniram Judson

Then, dipping his pen in ink, he wrote

'1st October 1835 -
Abigail Ann born.'

Leaving the ink to dry, he took a sheet of paper and wrote to his sister in America.

My dear Abigail, Today I have become the father of a daughter. Sarah was delivered of a healthy-looking girl in the early hours of this morning. We have called her after both you and Ann. She's Abigail Ann Judson. I pray that you and she will be spared to meet each other one day. I can still hardly take in that God has been good enough to bless me with a second happy marriage, and a second wife with a heart burdened for the people of Burma. And that he should bless us with a child after all our sadnesses - that quite overwhelms me. Please pray for us. Pray for Sarah, that she might be soon restored to strength, for Abigail Ann to be worthy of the two names she bears, and for me too,

Your unworthy brother, Adoniram.

Less than two years later the Bible was open at the same page and another name was added. '*Adoniram Brown, born 7th April, 1837*' and the following summer Elnathan was the new baby in the family.

Koo-chil was patient with the toddlers who climbed up the ladder to his cookhouse, though he lifted them gently down again to keep them out of harm's way. Maung Ing laughed at their antics and taught them Burmese baby games. And the Christian women were the best childminders any family could have had. They loved each new baby as it came along, and delighted in all their antics as they grew older.

'If it weren't for my dear Burmese friends, I'd get no work done at all,' Sarah told her husband one day, as they looked over a manuscript.

'Your *'Life of Christ'* will be a great help in our work,' he said, turning over the pages and looking at the lines of circular characters. 'It seems no time since I wouldn't have understood a word of this. I wouldn't even have known where one word stopped and another started!'

'Without God's help it would still be a mystery to both of us. We've so much to be thankful for.'

'That, I think, should be our motto,' Adoniram said. 'We've so much to be thankful for.'

When Sarah left the room he allowed his memory to range back over the years, especially to his time of deep depression. 'Even then,' he thought, 'God was with me. I couldn't feel his presence, and I should not like to go through it again, but he was there in the forest with me. I certainly do have much to be thankful to God for.'

At the beginning of 1839 Adoniram developed a cough that would not go away. Because it looked like tuberculosis, he was prescribed a sea voyage for his health and he set out on a trip to Calcutta. But some of his time there was spoken for. Sarah had a list of instructions. 'I've written down the children's measurements so that you can have clothes made for them. Remember to get new shoes for yourself and to have your watch repaired. And don't forget to visit the people on the list, and have you got the bundle of letters I've written to them?' Judson smiled at the ordinariness of it. 'I could be a businessman in America going to the city for a week,' he thought. 'But that couldn't be further from the truth.'

Although he was much the better for the voyage, and the cough didn't develop into tuberculosis, he was never able to preach as many sermons after that time of illness.

Despite having a house full of children (Henry was born on the last day of 1839) Adoniram Judson completed his translation of the Bible on 24th October 1840.

'At last,' he thought, 'I can devote my time to building up the church.'

He took charge of the local mission work, organising the activities of the Burmese Christians who were sent out each day after the morning meeting to all parts of Moulmein and the surrounding villages. It was work that appealed to Judson after his many years bent over translation. Consequently, a letter from his Mission Board did not particularly please him.

'We should be grateful if you would prepare a Burmese dictionary. This would make the best use of your vast knowledge of the language, and it would provide a most useful resource for future missionaries to your part of the world.'

Adoniram read the letter over and over again then discussed it with his wife.

'It seems to me to be such a chaotic affair, and very unmissionary.'

Sarah knew what he meant. 'But think how useful it would have been if a dictionary had been available when we came out to Burma.'

That swayed his thinking, and he undertook the task. That took most of his time over the following winter.

The spring of 1841 was not easy. Sarah and the children were poorly, and it was decided that the climate at Amherst would suit them better than staying in Moulmein over the hot season. Amherst, which was on the sea, was always a little cooler. But even there Sarah, Abigail and little Adoniram grew worse. Fearing for the lives of his loved ones, Judson arranged a passage to Calcutta. His whole family would, he thought, benefit from the sea voyage. But when their friends in Moulmein got a letter from Sarah, they discovered that the voyage had not all been plain sailing.

It was the season of the southwest monsoon,' she wrote. *'On the fourth night at sea the ship struck a sandbank. Everyone expected to drown. I shall never forget my feelings as I looked over the side of the vessel that night, and fancied ourselves with our poor sick, and almost dying children, launched on its stormy waves. I managed to fill a small trunk with things we might need on the lifeboat. However, the tide was rising, the captain tacked, and after about twenty minutes the ship floated free. You should have heard my song of praise! In spite of all the excitement of the voyage, the whole family improved in the sea air. Adoniram brought us here to Serampore, where he has rented us a nice dry house, right on the bank of the river. Our time here is doing us good.*

Although it was a healthier Judson family that returned to Moulmein in November, they came back without little Henry. He died while they were away.

The following year another child was born, they called him Henry Hall. And between his birth and that of his brothers Charles and Edward, Sarah worked on translating 'Pilgrim's Progress' into Burmese. But she knew her health was failing.

'How I long to see George again,' she said, thinking of the six-year-old who had gone to America and who was now sixteen.

'I think we should make preparations to go to see him,' her husband said. 'You need medical treatment we can't get here, and it's time the three oldest children were back in America for their education.'

Sarah's heart broke to leave her youngest children behind, Charles and Edward, but the thought of seeing George once again spurred her on. While Sarah's heart sang at the prospect of seeing her son again, her body rebelled at the effort. George never did see his mother. She died when the ship was anchored off St Helena, and was buried at sea.

As usual Adoniram recorded his feelings in his diary.

For a few days, in the solitude of my cabin, with my poor children crying around me, I abandoned myself to heartbreaking sorrow. But the promise of the Gospel came to my aid, and I anticipated a happy meeting with those I love whose bodies are resting at Amherst and St Helena.

Six weeks later their boat, the *SophiaWalker*, dropped anchor in Boston harbour.

The Golden Shore

'How long is it since you left America?' Abigail asked her father, as they arrived in Boston.

'It's thirty-three years, and I've not been back in all that long time.'

Abigail stopped to think about that. 'You'll not recognise anyone and nobody will know who you are.'

'It'll be like being invisible!' laughed Elnathan who, having been brought up as one of the few non Burmese in Moulmein, could only begin to imagine the delights of being anonymous.

But it was left to Abigail to sense her father's feelings.

'Your papa and mamma and brother have died since you left. Does that make you feel sad?'

Judson hugged his perceptive daughter. 'Yes, it does,' he said, 'though they died a long time ago. But your Aunt Abigail will be here to meet us, and she's longing to get to know her namesake.'

His daughter felt both shy and excited at the prospect of meeting the aunt after whom she'd been named.

Elnathan's dreams of anonymity were not to be.

'Who are all these people?' he asked, in a confused voice.

News reporters, magazine writers, church leaders and tag-along-with-the-crowd locals were all there to greet them. Judson glanced behind to see who it was they were all looking for.

His sister Abigail tried to explain. 'They're wanting to meet you, brother. Don't you know that you're something of a celebrity?'

The realisation which worked its way across Judson's face quickly turned to a mixture of embarrassment and horror.

'A celebrity?' he puzzled. 'But ... I'm just ... I'm just me.'

His sister took his arm and smiled into his confused face.

'We must get the children out of here,' he said urgently to her. 'The poor things have just lost their mother.'

An old and respected church leader saw what was happening and steered the new arrivals away from the crowd.

News soon spread about Sarah Judson's death and people were more thoughtful about what they expected of the famous missionary family. However, several meetings were held at which Adoniram was the guest speaker. Although it thrilled him to see from the vast crowds who gathered that missionary interest in America was alive and well, he was incredibly shy when it came to speaking to them. For thirty-three years he had worked with individuals and small groups of people. He was quite unprepared for the fuss his presence promoted, and his voice hardly reached to the edges of the big halls in which he was asked to speak.

Arrangements were made for the young boys to live with the couple who had brought up George Boardman. And the half-brothers were delighted to meet each other.

'I have something to show you,' the sixteen-year-old told the two younger boys, laying his memory box on the floor between them.

'This,' he said, showing them the smooth pebble, 'came from the edge of the Mootangai.'

Elnathan held it in his hand. It felt so familiar and comforting.

'It's from home,' he said softly, rubbing the pebble on his cheek.

'And this is the kind of quill I learned to write with,' George told them, taking out the short feather.

'We did too!' the boys said together.

Elnathan smoothed the feather. Somehow the quill seemed to link Burma and George in a warm way.

'And my little clay monkey was given to me by a school friend before I left,' George explained, holding the thing out to his brothers.

Neither took it. Both were scrabbling in their pockets, and both produced a similar clay monkey to show to George.

'Your friend is still in the mission compound,' Elnathan explained. 'He told us about your monkey and he made these for us. 'And he asked us to send you his love,' he said in a rush.

George's eyes misted over at the thought. 'I'm glad you're here,' he told the two boys. 'I still miss Burma. Will you tell me about Mamma?' he asked in a broken voice. 'I was so looking forward to seeing her.'

'I think we need to buy you some clothes,' Aunt Abigail said to her niece.

'May I come with you?' the girl asked.

'How else would we know what fitted?' her aunt laughed.

Abigail explained that her mamma had just given measurements to the sewing woman and clothes were made up for the children. 'But I'll enjoy being there when they're bought,' the girl said.

Her aunt smiled. 'I'll make sure you do.'

Although the two Abigails were far apart in age, they had a great deal to say to each other.

Aunt Abigail wanted to know all about Burma, and that's just what her niece most wanted to talk about. And the older woman, who had never met Sarah, asked a lot about her. Young Abigail, grieving the loss of her mother, found it helped to talk.

On a visit to his sister and daughter, Adoniram had them both laughing heartily.

'So I was walking along the road,' he said, 'when I came to a newsboy. Taking a newspaper, I smiled at the lad, made some comment, and was about to move on. I was puzzled when I realised he was waiting for something. Then it dawned on me that he was waiting to be paid! "Why!" I said to him, "I've been giving out free papers in Burma so long I'd no idea I needed to pay here!"You should have seen his face! And the man I was with was so embarrassed!'

The next time Judson visited the two Abigails, it was with sad news. He'd had a letter from Burma telling him that little Charles had died. He was one-and-a-half years old.

With the children settled in their new homes, Adoniram Judson was free to travel throughout America, meeting those who were interested in supporting and praying for mission work.

'This journey's taking ages,' he told his companion, as their train stopped yet again.

'I'm going to find out what's wrong,' the other man said, opening the door and jumping out on to the gravel where a group of officials were talking.

'There's been an accident,' he reported, when he climbed back aboard. 'We'll be here for some time.'

'If I'd known that I'd have brought a book,' Judson commented.

'Read this,' his companion suggested, handing him '*Trippings in Author Land*'. It's very popular just now.

Adoniram didn't notice time passing, and he hardly took in that the train had started again and that they were speeding their way towards their destination.

'Is the author a Christian?' he asked, when he had finished the book.

'Yes,' his friend said, 'though what she writes is not specifically Christian, just good wholesome stuff.'

Judson nodded. 'She writes brilliantly.'

His travelling companion laughed. 'You'll be able to tell her that yourself when we get home because she's staying with us just now!'

11th December, 1845

It's been a strange experience getting to know Emily Chubbock,' Adoniram wrote in his diary. 'All I knew about her was gleaned from her book which I read on the train on my way here - and that's written under an assumed name. Had my host not told me who she was I should not even have known she was an author, far less a well-known one! Although I knew nothing of Miss Chubbock, she knew a great deal about me. It seems that she has been interested in missions for some years and has followed news of the work in Burma with great interest. This became clear by the intelligent and perceptive questions she asked both about the church there and about the family. It is almost as though she had met us before!

'Would you consider writing a biography of Sarah?' Judson asked Miss Chubbock, while they were still at Philadelphia. 'You're the perfect person to do it because you know so much of her story already.'

'Thank you, Mr Judson,' the author answered. 'I'd count that a great privilege. Perhaps while we're here you could begin to tell me some details of her life.'

Mr Judson and Miss Chubbock spent a lot of time together in their friend's home, drafting the book and beginning to flesh out its contents.

Before long they were on first-name terms, and by the time Adoniram left Philadelphia they were firm friends and had a good understanding of each other's natures and situations.

On 20th January 1846, Adoniram wrote three letters. One was to Emily, inviting her to consider marriage. The second was to the two Abigails telling of his hopes and plans, and the third was to George, Adoniram and Elnathan. The children's replies were even more satisfactory that their father had hoped for. He hadn't realised that his intended had written one of their favourite books! But not everyone was pleased. A few people had, in their minds, made Judson into some kind of very special and different person, and his marrying again didn't fit into their strange ideas. But Adoniram was as human as God had made him, and he and Emily were ideally suited to each other. They were married at the beginning of June, and five weeks later they sailed for Burma.

We are having a good voyage,' Emily wrote to the two Abigails. *'Tonight we had a supper of dolphins, which, but for their being fried in rancid lard, would have been delicious. We are as busy as you can imagine. Part of the day is spent with your papa working on his dictionary and me ploughing my way through his Burmese grammar book, and for the remainder he teaches me the spoken language.*

It was November when the couple were rowed up the Irrawaddy to Moulmein and the welcome of welcomes. Having been a little concerned about how his two youngest sons would get on with their stepmother, it was with a sense of relief that he wrote to the boys in America. '*Of course we all miss Mamma, as you do too, but Emily is good to us, and the boys love her.*'

'As there are nearly thirty missionaries here,' Adoniram told a meeting in Moulmein, 'I think it would be worth considering me moving back to Rangoon to work. I could get on with the dictionary and Emily could continue with Sarah's biography. We could help to build up the church.'

'What about going for a short visit to see how things are there?'

Judson thought about it.

'That would be a good idea,' Emily encouraged. 'Then we could make an informed decision.'

When Judson arrived back with the news that it was safe to move, his wife had already started packing.

'I think we should call the mission house Bat Castle,' Emily suggested to the boys soon after they arrived in Rangoon. 'There are thousands of them living here!'

'And cockroaches,' Henry said.

'And lizards,' added Edward, 'and rats.'

Emily shuddered. 'I don't mind the lizards, but I'm not fond of rats.'

'What about the ants and mosquitoes and bedbugs?'

Henry asked. 'Do you like them?'

His stepmother laughed. 'They're better than rats, but we'd sleep sounder without the bedbugs!'

'You're making me scratch just listening to you!' Adoniram told his little family. 'Let's just be grateful we have a home, even if we do have to share it with some of the animal population of Rangoon!'

They shared it with people too. The Christians in Rangoon had scattered because of persecution and it took a great deal of courage for them to gather together in the mission house for meetings. But just seven months later, when it became too dangerous for them to associate with the missionaries at all, the Judsons packed up their few belongings and left Rangoon for the very last time. Had they not gone when they did, some of the believers would have lost their lives.

'It's the day before Christmas,' Edward told his older brother, 'and we've got a Christmas baby of our very own.'

He looked into the crib where the new Emily Judson was sucking her tiny hand.

'I wanted a little sister because I miss my big sister,' Henry said.

The following morning their father woke them as usual with a piece of Burmese cake.

'Don't drop any crumbs,' Adoniram told Edward. 'That's what encourages rats.'

'Were any caught in the trap last night?' Henry asked, as he did every morning.

'No, none,' their father told them. 'You must have eaten up every last crumb yesterday!'

'What's that?' Edward asked, seeing something sticking out of his father's hand.

'These are your presents,' laughed Adoniram. 'Had you forgotten it was Christmas?'

The boys jumped out of their bed and took the little clay monkeys from their father.

'Thank you!' they shouted excitedly. 'They're like the ones Adoniram and Elnathan took with them to America.'

'And your big brother George has one too. They've become something of a family tradition.'

The two years that followed were busy in a happy kind of a way. Adoniram finished the dictionary, all six hundred pages of it! Emily looked after the children and completed her biography of Sarah. Judson, whose voice was better than it had been for some time, enjoyed preaching. One of his favourite subjects was the golden shore, the gate of heaven. Of course the idea of heaven being golden appealed to the Burmese and they loved hearing sermons on it.

'Look at Mr and Mrs Judson,' a neighbour said. 'They're off!'

His wife came to watch. It was their morning entertainment. Adoniram ran right from the top of the hill near the mission compound. Emily waited until she saw him start running and she raced away from halfway down. The challenge for Adoniram was to catch her before she reached the bottom. The hill was steep, and they zigzagged down like mountain goats. He was sixty and she was half his age, but he nearly always won.

'He's very poorly,' Emily was told. 'It's dysentery.'

She held her husband's thin hand in hers. He was in a restless sleep, and she prayed at his side.

'Thank you Father, for the three happy years we've had together. If it's your will, please help Adoniram to recovery and bless us with more time together to serve your people here in Burma.'

'Amen,' said a weak voice from the bed. Judson had woken up and heard his wife's prayer.

'Amen,' they repeated together.

Their prayer was answered. Adoniram recovered sufficiently to go out for short horse rides with his wife. But everyone, including Emily, could see that he was still very ill. And he spent more and more time each day in prayer.

'The only hope for him is some clean sea air,' was the best advice they were given. 'It just *might* help him.'

Plans were made for a voyage.

'How I wish you could come with me,' Judson told his wife, 'but the baby is due too soon.'

Emily bit her lip. She knew he was dying.

The day before Adoniram was due to go she was reading a paper to him when she came upon news that thrilled her.

'Listen to this,' she said excitedly. 'Some Jews in

Trebizond have been converted through reading a tract published in Germany giving an account of your work in Ava!'

Adoniram's eyes lit up. 'Praise the Lord!' he said. 'I have so much to be thankful for.'

Emily Judson hired a small river-boat and watched as her husband was carried aboard. When she heard the next day that the ship was still tied up at Amherst, she hired a boat and went downriver to say her last farewell.

Two days later, just falling asleep at 4.15 pm on Friday 12th April 1850, Adoniram Judson died not far off the coast of Burma. The land he loved so much was behind him, the golden shore of heaven was in front, and he crossed from one to the other.

Thinking Further Topics

Chapter 1: Young Mr Judson

As a child Adoniram believed what his parents taught him, but as he grew up he became rebellious. Instead of discussing issues with his father and mother he took advice from his friends and rejected all he had been brought up to trust in.

Is it good to accept all that you are taught at home or should young people think for themselves? Do you feel pressured by what your friends think, sometimes giving in to them against your better judgment? It takes courage to stand up for what you believe.

Does the Bible have anything to say about practical things like these? Proverbs 23:19 - What does the Bible say about parental advice? Proverbs 1:8-10 - Have your parents warned you about peer pressure? 1 Corinthians 15:33. Proverbs 15:1 - Is there a right way of disagreeing?

Chapter 2: About turn!

It must have been hard for Adoniram to go home after he'd made a mess of his independence, but he did it all the same. Do you find it difficult to face the music? Do your parents always respond in the way you think they will? How much does their response depend on how you present your case?

When he became a Christian, Judson had to tell his parents. If you are a believer, did you find it difficult to tell your mother and father? Why do you think that was? Were you scared they might have too high expectations of you?

Perhaps you are a young Christian and your parents are not believers. Do you feel the need of more mature people to guide you? Is there anyone in your church you can talk to, or do you have friends whose parents are Christians?

Ephesians 6:1-4 - Parent /child relationships are a two-way thing.

1 Timothy 4:12 - Being a youthful believer has its privileges and its responsibilities.

1 Timothy 2:1-2 - Scripture tells us to pray for those in authority, and the authorities referred to were not Christians. Does this include non Christian parents? What else does this verse say that those under authority should be doing?

Chapter 3: Adventures at sea

Adoniram's sea experiences must have been very scary at the time. Do you have things and situations you're afraid of? How do you cope with fear? And if you have fears that seem silly to some other people, how do you cope with them?

Several times in this chapter Judson was in real danger. Have you ever been in danger? There are all kinds of dangers, not just accidents and pirates! Are you in danger of being offered drugs or alcohol? Are you in danger of going to places you'd be best not to go to, or of seeing films and videos that you know are harmful? How can you avoid dangers of that kind?

Isaiah 43:1-3 - Is there a promise here for us when we are fearful? Does it apply to times of danger too? What could 'the waters' and 'rivers' and 'fire' refer to? Are there times when we feel as though we are drowning in a problem, of being pulled deeper into a dangerous situation, or have we had our fingers severely burnt? Could these be examples of what Scripture is referring to?

Ephesians 6:10-18 - Is there protection available for us?

Ephesians 5:15-17 - Are some things in our own hands?

Chapter 4: La Belle Creol

When they were in America the little group of would-be missionaries got on well together and they planned to work as a team when they went abroad. But the Judsons changed their views on a theological subject and the group split up and went their different ways. Can we disagree with others and still work with them? Are there times when it's best to part company even with good friends with whom you hold much in common? And if disagreements are more trivial, is it possible to restore relationships to what they were before? If that can be done, how can you do it?

Although they disagreed and went in different directions, the young missionaries were all still serving God. Do disagreements spoil a Christian's witness? Or can a good resolution to a difficult problem actually be an example of Christian living?

Acts 15:36-40 - Even the apostles disagreed. How did they cope with it? Were they right?

2 Timothy 2:22-26 - Do verses 23-26 result from not taking the advice in v 22?

Ephesians 4:26 - Gives a time limit of 24 hours or less!

Chapter 5: Early days

Because Adoniram and Ann didn't want to be different from their Burmese friends they tried to fit in. How much should we fit in with the culture around us? Are there limits beyond which we shouldn't go? Or should we get right in there with the intention of being a Christian influence? What about in personal relationships? Has the Bible anything to say about relating to non-believers, or about dating someone who is not a Christian?

The Judsons lost their little son, Roger. Has someone you love died or gone away? It may be that divorce has meant that someone you love is no longer there for you. How do you deal with the hurt and pain of separation? Do you bottle it up? It's not wrong to cry. Jesus wept when his friend died.

Romans 12:2 - Can you think of any ways in which you are conforming to the pattern of the world, and ways in which these could be transformed? 2 Corinthians 6:14 - This is a big one. Does anyone marry someone they've never dated? What does that say about Christians dating unbelievers? Is that inequality? Matthew 11:28-30 - Jesus knows our burdens. What does he ask us to do with them? John 11:17-37 - Is Jesus really human? Does he really understand how we feel?

Chapter 6: Goings and comings

Some people are real worriers, if they have nothing to worry about they worry about that! Are you a worrier? Are your worries based on real fears or not? Do you analyse your worries to see if they have foundations? The Bible is a very practical book. Does it have anything to say about worry?

One Burmese woman who was interested in Christianity had a dreadful temper. Is anger always wrong? Is it sometimes right to be angry? Can anger get things done that a cool head and reason can't? What about keeping anger on the boil over a long period. Is that ever a good thing?

Matthew 6:25-34 - Is worry sometimes about priorities, comparisons and insecurities? Is the advice in verse 34 the bottom line on the subject?

2 Timothy 2:22-26 - Back to the subject of anger. Are temper and anger the same thing? If not, what's the difference?

Ephesians 4:26-27 - Why does verse 27 follow on from verse 26? What a warning!

Chapter 7: The Golden Presence

Adoniram was very disappointed in the outcome of his meeting with the king. Was he disappointed in how he had presented his case or in how the king reacted? How do you cope when you're disappointed with yourself? And how do you deal with disappointment with other people?

The Judsons were pleased that the new converts 'grew in grace,' that means that God made a difference to their lives. If you are a Christian, can others see changes in your life? Or are you still struggling to fit in with all your old friends and not allowing God's work to show? Growing in grace means becoming more like Jesus. Think about Jesus, and think of ways you want to become more like him. Becoming like Jesus is hard. Are there things in your life that you know are very unlike Jesus and that you really need to work on?

1 Timothy 4:15-16 - Is this practical advice that we can apply to ourselves? Romans 8:28-29 - What does this say about adverse situations? Can God use even them to make us more like Jesus? 1 John 3:1-3 - This is a wonderful promise? When will it come true?

Chapter 8: Ava, at last

The missionaries had very few converts to show for all the years they worked in Burma. Is success counted in numbers of converts? Should we be looking for big numbers in churches? Is big always beautiful? Are there advantages and disadvantages in big and small groups? In which are you more comfortable? If you're comfortable in a small group is it because you like closeness? If it's a big group you look for, is it because you can hide behind other people and not be noticed?

The Judsons brought up two little girls who had social problems? Are we prepared to get involved in messy issues or do we like dealing only with nice clean situations? What does the Bible have to say about helping others?

Matthew 18:20 - Is this a promise worth remembering when we feel down about small numbers?

Luke 15: 8-10 - What causes the angels in heaven to rejoice? How many sinners repenting does that take?

Matthew 25:31-46 - How should we help others? And why?

Chapter 9: Death Prison

Adoniram Judson went through terrible things in prison, and all of it because he was a Christian. Have you ever suffered for your faith? Have you ever been persecuted because you believe in Jesus? What is persecution? Can it mean being laughed at, missing out on invitations, being scorned? Or does the word persecution only apply to things like being in prison?

God was with Adoniram in prison but that didn't lessen his pain or suffering. So what difference does being a Christian make when you have problems? Is the knowledge that Jesus also suffered a help when the going is tough? Does he really understand what we are going through?

Matthew 5:10-12 - Can persecution be a blessing to us even though we don't feel it at the time? Was that true of Adoniram Judson? Is it possible to rejoice under persecution? Did Judson rejoice at any time in prison?

Mark 15:16-20 - Does Jesus understand what it feels like to be persecuted? Read Luke 23:26-49 to see the depths of his understanding, and all from personal experience.

Chapter 10: Oung-pen-la

Some time after Ann's death Adoniram suffered from severe depression. Do you ever get down? Is there a difference between feeling low and being depressed? If you really felt depressed would you ask for help? Who would you go to? Would you look for a Christian to help you or would you go to your doctor? Depending on what causes depression, doctors can help a great deal. Some people feel guilty about being depressed, especially Christians. Do you think that's appropriate? Or is depression part of being human?

Does the Bible have anything to say on the subject of depression?

1 Kings 19:1-9 -With God's help Elijah had just challenged all the prophets of Baal and had seen them defeated. Then he went into a state of depression. God knew what he needed and it was two practical things. What were they? (vs 5 and 7). Sometimes depression has physical causes. Food and sleep may help, but so might medication.

Psalm 13 - David was depressed from time to time. When he was depressed did he think it would pass? (v 1-2). What was his prayer? (v 3). And what did he do when his depression was lifted? (v 5-6).

Chapter 11: A second happiness

Marriage was very precious to Adoniram Judson. His first and second wives died, and he was in fact married three times. It may be that you come from a happy home and know from the inside what a good marriage is about. But you may come from a broken home or have seen your parents divorce. Do you think your experience will colour your future relationships? If you've had a rough time will you still aim for a marriage

153

that lasts? Do you see divorce as a speedy way out of an uncomfortable situation, or do you intend to put effort into your marriage and make it work?

The Bible has a lot to say about marriage - that's because God invented it! Have you thought about Biblical marriage?

Genesis 2:18 - Why did God make a companion for Adam?

Genesis 2:22-25 - This is the first marriage! If God made marriage what does that say about those who destroy it?

Ephesians 5:22-33 - make a list of the biblical ground rules for marriage.

Chapter 12: The Golden Shore

Judson's friend, Jacob Eames, was not ready to die. Was Adoniram ready to go when his time came? What makes someone ready to die? Are old people ready to die and young people not, or is there more to it than that? One of the people the writer has known who was most ready to die when the Lord called him was just fifteen years old. Do you assume you'll grow old and have time to prepare for death? What's the basis of that assumption?

What happens after death? Does everyone go to heaven regardless of how they lived or what they believe? Is there a universal happy ending?

Psalm 89:48 - What does this say about death?

Matthew 25:46 - Does Jesus give any hope of a universal happy ending?

Philippians 1:21-24 - Why did Paul long for heaven? But what made him content to remain on earth?

Revelation 21:1-4 - Does this explain why Adoniram looked forward to heaven?

Adoniram Judson
Time Line

1788	Adoniram born in Malden, Massachusetts.
1799	George Washington dies at Mount Vernon.
1800	The U. S. capital is moved from Philadelphia to Washington, D.C.
1801	The Kingdom of Great Britain and the Kingdom of Ireland merge to form the United Kingdom.
1804	Entered Brown University.
1808	Entered Andover Theological Seminary.
1810	Helped form the American Board of Commissioners for Foreign Missions.
1812	Adoniram and his new wife, Ann, sailed for India, but were refused entry and went to Burma where they worked for six years.
1812	America at war with Britain and Canada.
1813	First child born dead and buried at sea.
1815	Roger born. Napoleon defeated at Waterloo.
1816	Roger died.
1821	New York gives free Blacks the right to vote.
1824	Mexico becomes a republic – outlaws slavery.
1824-25	Adoniram imprisoned.
1825	Maria born.
1826	Ann Judson died.
1827	Maria died.
1833	Slavery Abolition Act bans slavery throughout the British Empire.

1834	Adoniram marries Sarah Boardman.
1835	Abigail Ann born.
1835-36	The Texas Revolution in Mexico resulted in the short-lived Republic of Texas.
1838-40	Civil war in the Federal Republic of Central America.
1840	Adoniram completed the Burmese Bible after 23 years.
1844	Samuel Morse sends first telegraph message from Washington to Baltimore
1845	Returned for a visit to America. Sarah died.
1846	Adoniram married Emily Chubbock and returns to Burma.
1846-47	Mormon migration to Utah.
1848	Start of the California Gold Rush.
1849	Adoniram completed the Burmese-English Dictionary which is still used today.
1850	Adoniram died en route to France and was buried at sea.

THE TRAILBLAZER SERIES

Corrie ten Boom, The Watchmaker's Daughter
ISBN 978-1-85792-116-8

Bill Bright, Dare to be Different
ISBN 978-1-85792-945-4

Adoniram Judson, Danger on the Streets of Gold
ISBN 978-1-85792-660-6

Amy Carmichael, Rescuer by Night
ISBN 978-1-85792-946-1

Billy Graham, Just Get up out of Your Seat
ISBN 978-1-84550-095-5

Isobel Kuhn, Lights in Lisuland
ISBN 978-1-85792-610-1

C.S. Lewis, The Storyteller
ISBN 978-1-85792-487-9

Martyn Lloyd-Jones, From Wales to Westminster
ISBN 978-1-85792-349-0

George Müller, The Children's Champion
ISBN 978-1-85792-549-4

Robert Murray McCheyne, Life is an Adventure
ISBN 978-1-85792-947-8

John Newton, A Slave Set Free
ISBN 978-1-85792-834-1

John Paton, A South Sea Island Rescue
ISBN   978-1-85792-852-5

Helen Roseveare, On His Majesty's Service
ISBN 978-1-84550-259-1

Mary Slessor, Servant to the Slave
ISBN 978-1-85792-348-3

Joni Eareckson Tada, Swimming against the Tide
ISBN 978-1-85792-833-4

Hudson Taylor, An Adventure Begins
ISBN 978-1-85792-423-7

William Wilberforce, The Freedom Fighter
ISBN 978-1-85792-371-1

Richard Wurmbrand, A Voice in the Dark
ISBN 978-1- 85792-298-1

Gladys Aylward, No Mountain too High
ISBN: 9781857925944

Michael Farraday, Spiritual Dynamo
ISBN: 9781845501563

Charles Spurgeon, Prince of Preachers
ISBN: 9781845501556

CHRISTIAN FOCUS PUBLICATIONS

Christian Focus | Christian Heritage | CF4K | Mentor

Christian Focus Publications publishes books for adults and children under its four main imprints: Christian Focus, CF4K, Mentor and Christian Heritage. Our books reflect that God's word is reliable and Jesus is the way to know him, and live for ever with him.

Our children's publication list includes a Sunday school curriculum that covers pre-school to early teens; puzzle and activity books. We also publish personal and family devotional titles, biographies and inspirational stories that children will love.

If you are looking for quality Bible teaching for children then we have an excellent range of Bible story and age specific theological books.

From pre-school to teenage fiction, we have it covered!

**Find us at our web page:
www.christianfocus.com**

CF4•K
Because you're never
too young to know Jesus